Milwaukee Road Remembered is dedicated to all the people who in their daily lives performed the myriad duties necessary to operate the Chicago, Milwaukee, St. Paul & Pacific and its predecessors.

Time freight 263 rolls through Hoyt Park in Wauwatosa, Wisconsin, behind 4-8-4 No. 238, on May 13, 1949. — *Jim Scribbins*.

MILWAUKEE ROAD REMEMBERED

A fresh look at an unusual railroad

BY JIM SCRIBBINS

Library of Congress Catalog Card Number 89-080800.

ISBN: 0-89024-075-2.

Front endpaper: Train 21, the *Chippewa-Hiawatha* between Plymouth and Elkhart Lake, Wisconsin. — *John Sachse*. Back endpaper: A three-unit F7 leads a freight train through Canton, South Dakota, in November 1956. — *Jim Scribbins*.

EDITOR: George H. Drury
COPY EDITOR: Marcia Stern
ART DIRECTOR: Lawrence Luser

CONTENTS

WHY REMEMBER THE MILWAUKEE ROAD?

In the better years of railroading, all roads had certain individual characteristics, but some companies displayed more personality than others. The Milwaukee Road was one of those.

The road's shops at Milwaukee built fleets of steam locomotives and pioneered all-welded freight and passenger car construction. The Milwaukee Road designed the first North American 4-6-4, which accepted 914-mile runs as commonplace. Mechanical engineers at the shops also planned the first streamlined steam locomotives intended for sustained 100 mph speeds. Milwaukee operated the fastest scheduled steam-powered trains anywhere in the world.

The Milwaukee Road proved the feasibility of long-distance movement of heavy trains by electricity on its Puget Sound Extension, which crossed five mountain ranges in Montana, Idaho, and Washington. Diesel diversity was present, too, with all major builders except Lima-Hamilton represented.

For the most part, the Milwaukee Road operated its own sleeping cars, and the few Pullman-operated sleepers had their bedding inscribed with the road's initials. Contrasting with the sterling *Hiawathas* and the "Rolls-Royce of American Railroading," as the 1927 edition of the *Pioneer Limited* was described, were mixed trains with sleeping cars and streamlined, open-platform, kerosene-lit combines.

For years the average speed of the road's Chicago-Milwaukee passenger service was better than a mile a minute, with many of the trains making the 85-mile trip in 75 minutes. On how many other railroads did passenger trains regularly use diesel, electric, and steam propulsion in the course of their journeys as the *Olympian Hiawatha* and *Columbian* did?

In addition to the places one would expect to find them, the road had tunnels in Wisconsin and Indiana and helper grades in Iowa and Illinois. It possessed pontoon (floating) bridges across the Mississippi and Missouri rivers at four locations.

In the pages of this book, you'll find many other reasons to remember the Milwaukee Road.

JIM SCRIBBINS

Milwaukee, Wisconsin
June 1989

The Milwaukee Road used pontoon bridges to cross the Mississippi River at Prairie du Chien, Wisconsin, and Wabasha, Minnesota, and to cross the Missouri at Chamberlain and Mobridge, South Dakota. The rear cars of this freight train are on the floating portion of the bridge that spans the Mississippi's east channel at Prairie du Chien. One end of that portion of the bridge is hinged to the stationary part and can be swung through 90 degrees to open a channel for river shipping. — *John H. Gruber.*

Train 33 rolls off the west pontoon of the Prairie du Chien bridge into Marquette, Iowa. A steam-powered mechanism could raise and lower the deck of the bridge in relation to the level of the river and also move the floating part of the bridge out of the way of river traffic. — Cecil Cook.

Milwaukee & St. Paul No. 39, a 4-4-0 named *E. M. Hall*, stands in front of the depot-hotel at Portage, Wisconsin. The locomotive was originally on the roster of the Milwaukee & Watertown, which was opened in 1855 and consolidated with the La Crosse & Milwaukee in 1856. The La Crosse & Milwaukee became the Milwaukee & St. Paul in 1863.

A BRIEF HISTORY OF THE MILWAUKEE ROAD

In the 1840s Milwaukee had already become the largest city in the territory of Wisconsin, primarily because of its location on the shore of Lake Michigan. The Great Lakes provided the major transportation link, albeit a circuitous one, between the East and the upper Midwest. Milwaukeeans, eager to keep their city ahead of other Wisconsin ports and on a par with rapidly growing Chicago, flirted briefly with the idea of a canal west to the Rock River to link Lake Michigan with the Mississippi and open the interior of Wisconsin. Then they realized a railroad would be better.

The Milwaukee & Waukesha Rail Road was chartered in 1847, the year before Wisconsin achieved statehood. The proposed road, which was to run about twenty miles west from the shore of Lake Michigan, removed the last lingering thoughts of canals.

In the ensuing two years Milwaukee's population doubled, to 21,000, while that of the new state almost quadrupled. In the spring of 1849, the Milwaukee & Waukesha was formally organized under a revised charter allowing it to extend beyond Waukesha to Madison and thence to the Mississippi River. Byron Kilbourn, mayor of Milwaukee, was president of the company.

In February 1850, the company's title was changed to Milwaukee & Mississippi. The first rails were spiked down September 12, 1850. Five miles of track were opened to Wauwatosa on November 20, 1850. Motive power was an 1848 Norris-built 4-4-0 named *Bob Ellis*. (History has not recorded the significance of Ellis.)

Formal opening of the line to Waukesha occurred February 25, 1851, and featured all of the customary celebrating. The line reached Madison, the state capital, via a circuitous route through Whitewater and Stoughton, in 1854, and Prairie du Chien, on the Mississippi River, three years later. Through passenger service to and from Chicago was established with the Chicago & North Western, but it is unclear whether the junction was at Janesville, at the end of a Milwaukee & Mississippi branch, or at Milton.

Differences of opinion within the management, particularly with regard to finances, led to the termination of Kilbourn's presidency. Kilbourn surfaced as president of the newly organized La Crosse & Milwaukee Rail Road in summer 1852 only to resign under financially related pressure a year before the cross-state route was completed. The La Crosse & Milwaukee built from Milwaukee through Horicon and Portage to La Crosse between 1854 and 1858.

Within a relatively short time two railroads had been constructed across the state between Milwaukee and the Mississippi River, assuring Milwaukee's future. The desirability of extending both roads beyond Wisconsin was recognized even as both roads fleshed themselves out within the state. A complicated series of events involving mortgages, bankruptcies, and sales intervened. To simplify: The La Crosse & Milwaukee became the Milwaukee & St. Paul, which gained control of the Milwaukee & Prairie du Chien, successor to the Milwaukee & Mississippi, then fully absorbed it at the end of 1867.

11

Prominent in all of this was Milwaukee banker Alexander Mitchell, considered by many to be the Milwaukee Road's greatest chief executive.

During 1866 the McGregor Western Railway built northwest from McGregor, Iowa, across the Mississippi from Prairie du Chien, to Cresco, Iowa. Another company, the Minnesota Central Railway, built south from Minneapolis and St. Paul to Owatonna, Minn., between 1864 and 1866. In 1867 it was acquired by the McGregor Western. Less than two months later the McGW was acquired by the Milwaukee & St. Paul, which promptly closed the gap between Cresco and Owatonna, creating in November of that year a through line between Milwaukee and the Twin Cities, and in connection with the Chicago & North Western south of Milton, Wis., a through rail route between Chicago and the growing Minnesota cities.

It became obvious M&StP needed its own access to Chicago. Moreover, a route up the Mississippi valley north of La Crosse would create a Milwaukee-Twin Cities route 80 miles shorter than the line through Prairie du Chien and Owatonna. Between 1869 and 1872, the St. Paul & Chicago Railway, originally a segment of the St. Paul & Pacific, the ancestor of the Great Northern, built along the Minnesota bank of the Mississippi between St. Paul and La Crescent, opposite La Crosse. For a while it appeared that StP&C, after it was cut adrift from the future northern transcontinental, would become an extension of the Chicago & North Western system. The La Crosse, Trempealeau & Prescott in 1870 bridged the Mississippi at Winona. The Milwaukee & St. Paul had its eye on that line, which became part of the Chicago & North Western, but gained a larger prize instead, the St. Paul & Chicago, in 1872. However, until opening its own bridge at La Crosse in November 1876, M&StP trains used the Winona bridge.

On February 1, 1873, the Milwaukee & St. Paul opened a line from Milwaukee to Chicago, and a year later the railway added "Chicago" to its name.

Under Mitchell and his successor, Roswell Miller, the Chicago, Milwaukee & St. Paul became a major rail system. Extensions were built by the railroad itself, or accomplished through acquisition. The Southern Minnesota Railroad built from La Crescent, Minn., west into Dakota Territory between 1866 and 1879. The Hastings & Dakota Railway, most of which ultimately became part of the Milwaukee's Pacific Coast route, built across Minnesota during those years. Both names were perpetuated as CM&StP operating divisions.

The Puget Sound Extension was built late enough that powered earth-moving and track-laying machinery could be used in its construction. The Kelly Creek bridge is shown under construction in December 1908. — W. B. Lazear.

The Western Union Railroad (its final independent name) was a line from Racine, Wis., across southern Wisconsin and northern Illinois to the Mississippi at East Moline. It was built between 1855 and 1866 and was leased to the CM&StP in 1879, becoming its Racine & Southwestern Division. In 1880 the CM&StP leased Chicago & Pacific Railroad, which had a line from Chicago to Byron, Ill., and extended it west to meet the Racine & Southwestern Division at Kittredge, a few miles east of Lanark, Ill. These two routes became stepping stones for the Milwaukee's next major expansion.

During the 1870s the Milwaukee gained control of several railroads in eastern Iowa. By 1880 the system reached into Iowa as far as Marion and Cedar Rapids. The road bridged the Mississippi between Savanna, Ill., and Sabula, Iowa, in 1881, and in 1882 it reached the western border of Iowa at Council Bluffs, the eastern terminus of the Union Pacific. (The Milwaukee Road first reached the Missouri River in 1879 at Running Water on the Dakota Territory-Nebraska border.)

The road reached the Missouri for the third time when it completed a line to Kansas City in 1887. A cutoff from Davenport to Ottumwa considerably shortened the roundabout route through Marion in 1903, the year the road introduced the *Southwest Limited*.

During the remaining years of the nineteenth century the Chicago, Milwaukee & St. Paul fleshed out its route structure in the upper Midwest and became a blue-chip property. It even reached into James J. Hill's province by completing a line to Fargo, Dakota Territory, in 1885. The last major independent carrier it acquired was the Milwaukee & Northern in 1893, a line from Milwaukee to the upper peninsula of Michigan.

Mitchell died in 1887. Control of the St. Paul began to drift away from Milwaukeeans and Scottish banks and came into the sphere of the Rockefeller (Standard Oil) and Armour (meat packing) interests. The general offices were moved from Milwaukee to Chicago in 1890.

The Milwaukee Road's management felt expansion was necessary to stay competitive with the Great Northern, Northern Pacific, and Chicago, Burlington & Quincy, which were under common control. It considered extensions from Kansas City and Omaha to California, and from the Missouri River in South Dakota to Seattle and Tacoma. In November 1905 the road announced its intention to build through the Northwest to Puget Sound.

Where the last spike of the Puget Sound Extension was driven between Garrison and Gold Creek, Montana, the Milwaukee Road erected a monument, a large spike painted yellow. The location of the last spike of the parallel Northern Pacific (1883) was only a mile or two away. — *Milwaukee Road.*

13

On October 30, 1955, Union Pacific moved its *City* streamliners from the Chicago & North Western to the Milwaukee Road for the Council Bluffs-Chicago segment of their runs. The eastbound *City of Portland* is shown at Davis Junction, Illinois, on the first day of operation over the Milwaukee Road. — *Jim Scribbins*.

By 1920 the Milwaukee Shops, teeming with activity, occupied much of the Menomonee River Valley west of downtown Milwaukee.

15

In 1961 the Milwaukee Road upgraded its Chicago suburban service with stainless steel bilevel coaches and Electro-Motive E9s. A train of bilevels is shown approaching Chicago Union Station, being pushed by an FP7, while the *Afternoon Hiawatha* departs for Minneapolis on the next track.
— *Mike Schafer.*

Construction was started from several locations by various companies which later were grouped together as the Chicago, Milwaukee & Puget Sound Railway. The Missouri River bridge gave the initial point of the extension its name: Mobridge. A fortunate bit of luck enabled the company to acquire the Montana Railroad, and the road also acquired several local railroads to fill out the system's route structure in the state of Washington. The extension was completed in May 1909 and formally became part of CM&StP in 1912. At the same time the Milwaukee Road undertook another westward extension from the Missouri River — from Chamberlain to Rapid City, S. Dak., completed in 1907.

Difficulties with winter operations and with forest fires brought about the electrification of 656 route miles of the Pacific extension. Electricity was an efficient form of energy, but it was enormously expensive because the expected traffic volumes never materialized — and construction of the extension cost far more than anticipated.

The Chicago, Terre Haute & Southeastern Railway and the Chicago, Milwaukee & Gary Railway came into the Milwaukee family in 1921 and 1922, respectively, largely to give the road access to the coalfields of Indiana for lo-

comotive fuel. Financial burdens resulting from the extension to the Pacific and its electrification and from acquisition of the Southeastern and the Gary catapulted the Milwaukee Road in 1925 into the largest industrial bankruptcy up to that time.

The road was reorganized as Chicago, Milwaukee, St. Paul & Pacific Railroad in January 1928, only to go under again seven years later, just a month after the first *Hiawatha* took to the rails. However, that difficult era vigorously demonstrated the remarkable esprit de corps which existed on the Milwaukee Road and which seemed to become all the more steadfast under economic adversity. The *Hiawatha* was a stunning success. Its Atlantic and Hudson locomotives won worldwide acclaim. The Milwaukee Shops under the guidance of Karl F. Nystrom set the pace for the industry in all-welded passenger and freight car construction. The road introduced a fleet of fine dual-service 4-8-4 steam locomotives. It was evident that there was a "Milwaukee way" of doing things.

The road emerged from receivership amid the postwar optimism of December 1945. The *Hiawatha* trains were re-equipped and expanded. A new diesel locomotive shop was opened at Milwaukee as part of the dieselization

Milwaukee Road's new station in Milwaukee is shown the day it opened, August 4, 1965, with the *Morning Hiawatha*. It was the last major station constructed in the U. S. before Amtrak took over the nation's rail passenger service. It is notable for its train shed, which spans five tracks.
— *Jim Scribbins*.

program, completed for all practical purposes by early 1956. Even the electrification benefited from new locomotives received as a side effect of deteriorating international relations.

Like all railroads, the Milwaukee lost traffic to modes of transportation which were subsidized. Even at the same time it became the eastern link for Union Pacific's *City* streamliners in the mid-1950s, it was making major passenger train service reductions. However, in the early 1960s it thoroughly modernized Chicago suburban passenger service and constructed a new station in Milwaukee. The quality of Milwaukee Road's passenger service remained high until the establishment of Amtrak in 1971.

Intermodal service came to the Milwaukee Road with the adoption of Flexivan containers, but it didn't grow until the road changed to the more common practice of hauling regular highway trailers. CMSTP&P set the pace between the Midwest and Puget Sound when expedited time freight service was instituted in 1963. Its use of diesels for the entire distance (albeit with electric helpers) forecast the end of electrification on the Coast Division in 1971 and on the Rocky Mountain Division three years later.

During the 1950s and 1960s attempts were made to merge the Milwaukee with the Chicago & North Western; there was also a tentative look at merger with the Chicago, Rock Island & Pacific.

The Milwaukee experienced short-term gains resulting from mergers of other roads in its territory. It gained entry into Portland, Oregon, in 1971 and Louisville, Kentucky, in 1973 by trackage rights. Unfortunately, neither strengthened the road financially.

The Milwaukee Road always seemed to be struggling for prosperity and never attained it. The odds were overwhelming, and on December 19, 1977, the Milwaukee voluntarily entered reorganization. Trustees and management found two-thirds of its routes could not support themselves. Massive abandonments, including that of the Puget Sound Extension, were approved with the goal of saving that portion of the road for which there was genuine economic need.

Three other railroads competed for the slimmed-down, viable Milwaukee Road: the Grand Trunk Western, the Chicago & North Western, and the Soo Line. In February 1985 Soo Line Railroad acquired the Milwaukee Road's operating assets, and on January 1, 1986, the Soo merged the Milwaukee Road.

17

THE HIAWATHAS

In 1932, before streamlining had become commonplace, the Chicago, Milwaukee, St. Paul & Pacific — perhaps energized by the new Hudsons acquired during the previous two years — began to study the possibilities of passenger car weight reduction and improvements in passenger comfort. Largely under the genius of Karl Nystrom, chief mechanical officer, and Charles Bilty, mechanical engineer, the road developed what became the 4400 series coaches — the first full-size all-welded streamlined coaches on any railroad.

The first step leading ultimately to the *Hiawatha*s seems to have been a proposal for coaches which, except for their oval windows, were essentially identical to the forthcoming 4400s. Next were two experimental coaches of early 1934, cars 4000 and 4400. The former, rebuilt from sleeping car *Great Falls*, retained its clerestory roof and six-wheel trucks, but its interior and smooth exterior sides were identical to those of fully streamlined coach 4400.

The first motor-powered streamlined trains were delivered in 1934: Union Pacific's *M-10000* in February and Burlington's *Zephyr* in April of that year. They quickly created national interest in streamlining and speed, and the Milwaukee decided to capitalize on both. In April it authorized the building of 40 new coaches and 8 dormitory-coaches, the latter for the *Olympian*. (Only a few other railroads — New Haven and Boston & Maine for example — entered the streamline era by ordering large numbers of coaches for general service rather than a pride-of-the-line first-class train.)

In July 1934, Hudson 6402 took train 29 from Chicago to Milwaukee in 67½ minutes, averaging 75.5 mph and reaching a maximum speed of 103.5 mph. The train actually ran as the second section of the preceding train, No. 27, to allow operation ahead of its 90-minute schedule. Coach 4000 was in the consist — and meanwhile, car 4400, designated the "Progress Coach," was a hit at the Chicago World's Fair.

The next month, Burlington stated it would place *Zephyr*-type articulated diesel trains in service between Chicago and Minneapolis as soon as they could be manufactured by the Budd Company. At the same time the Milwaukee Road and the Chicago & North Western made known their intent to operate equally fast service between Chicago and the Twin Cities. The Milwaukee was well along in its streamlined coach program, and only feature cars needed to be planned in detail and built.

Given 1934 diesel technology, only steam was deemed capable of pulling the train to which CMStP&P was firmly committed: a full-size, non-articulated train, and those attributes were to play a positive role in its exceptional success. During the planning stage even extremely hefty 4-4-0s were considered, and drawings and sketches indicate that Lima Locomotive Works suggested a 4-4-4. American Locomotive Company won out with a pair of Atlantics, 4-4-2s so large they exceeded dimensions of many Pacifics. They were ordered in October 1934 for May 1935 delivery.

The Chicago & North Western upgraded conventional locomotives and

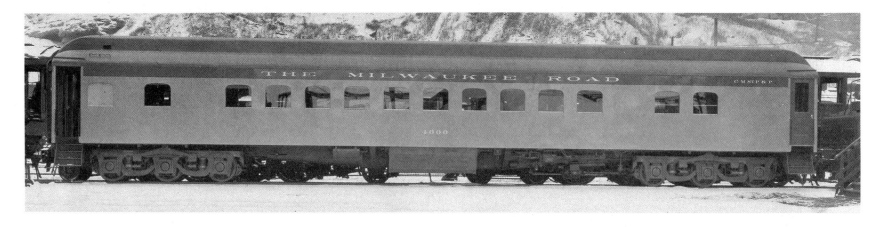

The innovation and craftsmanship of the Milwaukee Shops are evident in coach 4000, which was rebuilt from sleeping car *Great Falls* in February 1934. The car was notable for welded sides, though it retained its clerestory roof and six-wheel trucks. The interior (below) was identical to that of prototype streamlined coach 4400, built at the same time (except for the lights in the center of the ceiling, which weren't repeated on "production run" coaches). — *Both photos, Milwaukee Road.*

cars to put its *400* on the rails January 2, 1935. CB&Q's *Twin Zephyrs* entered service April 21, each of two trains making a single trip daily; on June 2, schedules were changed so that each made a round trip daily. After test runs and demonstration trips for media and public, the *Hiawatha* made its inaugural trip May 29, 1935.

The Milwaukee Road's new train was named the *Hiawatha* because the city of Winona, Minnesota, and Minnehaha Falls in Minneapolis were closely associated with characters in the famed Longfellow poem, and the legendary Indian could outrun an arrow he had shot, an apt symbol of the train's speed. Indian names for the parlor cars of the first two editions of the *Hiawatha* continued the theme.

The Milwaukee Road anticipated it would gain only overflow business from the *400* and the *Zephyr* and originally thought four or five cars would suffice, but trains 100 and 101 entered service with six-car consists. The class A 4-4-2s were designed to pull six cars and proved capable of handling nine cars at sustained 90-100 mph speeds.

The *Hiawatha* introduced the terms "Beaver Tail" and "Tip Top Tap" to the railroad's lexicon. (The Tip Top Inn was a restaurant on the top floor of the Pullman office building in Chicago.) The Milwaukee Road had painted its passenger cars orange and maroon ever since it had changed from varnished wood, so the exterior of the *Hiawatha* did not represent as marked a visual change as did streamliners on other railroads. Engines 1 and 2, though, made onlookers stare. They were not painted traditional steam-locomotive black. At Bilty's insistence, the orange and maroon colors were carried forward from the passenger cars to the pilots of the locomotives; industrial de-

Before it entered service, the original *Hiawatha* was displayed at cities along the route. People thronged to view the train on May 19, 1935, near the Minnesota Transfer roundhouse in the Midway area of St. Paul. — *Milwaukee Road: Harland's Camera Graphics.*

signer Otto Kuhler suggested the battleship-gray flanks of the shrouding above the running boards.

The *Hiawatha* was an immediate success and remained so until the Interstate highway era. The first trips were run with a Tip Top Tap diner, three coaches, parlor, and Beaver Tail parlor. In mid-June a fourth coach was added, and a fifth in August. Well over 16,000 passengers rode during the first six weeks — but they did not save the CMStP&P from declaring bankruptcy on June 29, 1935.

Financial misfortune did not cancel out passenger optimism. Because of its continuing success, the *Hiawatha* was awarded a completely new set of passenger cars on October 11, 1936. This "1937" train incorporated a full diner seating 48 in the middle of the train. The first car contained a sealed Railway Express room and a Tip Top Tap room seating 40. The demand for parlor seating was greater than had been anticipated, so a third parlor car with a drawing room was added, but to keep the train within the nine-car limit of the Atlantics, one coach was removed. Improvements were made in passenger comfort, mechanics, and esthetics of this second-edition *Hiawatha.*

Astoundingly, yet a third version of the *Hiawatha* took to the rails September 19, 1938, one connoisseurs frequently describe as the finest. It was joined January 21, 1939, by the *Morning Hiawatha*, trains 5 and 6, a vastly improved successor to the *Day Express*. Trains 100 and 101 were renamed the *Afternoon Hiawatha*. The morning and afternoon trains were identical in point of passenger luxury, but 5 and 6 carried a full Railway Post Office car. In addition, train 5 was given the task of carrying substantial quantities of parcels and packages for the Railway Express Agency, and Wisconsin's Public Service Commission required train 5 to make several additional stops. Because of the heavier consists, the *Morning Hiawatha* in both directions required an F7-class 4-6-4 up front — the Atlantics continued to work the other *Hiawatha* schedules from time to time. The high-drivered Hudsons carried chrome plates affixed to the shrouding over their cylinders acknowledging Otto Kuhler's magnificent styling. Kuhler was also responsible for the third and final Beaver Tail parlors which featured fins and immense glass windows affording an unsurpassed view to the rear.

During spring and summer of 1942, a number of new cars which had been authorized before the U. S. entered World War Two quietly entered service. New coaches went to both Twin Cities *Hiawathas*, with fleet leaders 100 and 101 also gaining new diners and new-style mid-train Tip Top Taps emphasizing snack meals as well as beverages.

In September 1941 diesel power came to the *Hiawatha* in the form of EMD E6 No. 15, which was assigned to train 6, the eastbound *Morning Hi.* For some years No. 6 was the road's fastest train, and between Sparta and Por-

Even though the streamlined Hudsons arrived a few weeks ahead of the "1939" cars, the engines did not run regularly on the *Afternoon Hiawatha* until passenger loadings increased substantially in 1940. The *Hiawatha* that was "ahead of its time" is shown on its third trip, September 21, 1938. According to the clock on the tower, the train has arrived well in advance of its 2:15 schedule. — *Milwaukee Road.*

tage, Wisconsin, it held the second fastest timing in the world. (Train 100's 4-6-4 maintained world steam speed leadership with its dash between New Lisbon and Portage.) In November 1941 CMStP&P's only Alco road diesel, DL-109 No. 14, was assigned to westbound *Hi* No. 101 as half of the diesel's daily Chicago-Minneapolis round trip.

Fifteen-car *Hiawatha* consists became the norm, but there was no serious compromise with quality. Some of the earlier coaches of 1934, 1937, and

1939 were used, but non-streamlined cars never appeared on main line *Hiawathas*, even during the trying wartime years.

Electro Motive E7s bumped the Hudsons and the DL-109 from *Hiawatha* service in 1946, and the Twin Cities *Hiawathas* received new cars again in 1948. Trains 5 and 6 inherited the 1942 tap cars from train 100 and 101, but everything else was new. The Skytop Lounge parlors became the trains' trademark. The only significant changes to the Twin Cities *Hiawathas* thereafter

(Left) A *Hiawatha* trainset spent an entire day on display in Milwaukee's Everett Street station. The station was opened in 1887, succeeding a station on Second Street south of the Menomonee River, and it was closed in 1965 when the present station opened a block south on St. Paul Avenue, close to the site of the original Milwaukee & Mississippi station of 1850. — *Milwaukee Road.*

Spectators have driven up to watch the proceedings as a train of 1948 *Hiawatha* equipment is halted at Morton Grove, Illinois, for a line-side portrait. The E7s heading the train will in a few months trade their gray-and-orange livery for one that matches the train. — *Milwaukee Road.*

The second diesel assigned to the *Hiawatha* was Alco DL-109 No. 14, shown here rounding a curve in Wauwatosa, Wisconsin, sometime during World War Two. The locomotive has acquired its second paint scheme and lost the grilles over its radiator shutters. Next stop: Portage, 86 miles and 69 minutes away. — *Milwaukee Road.*

24

were the Super Domes, which replaced the full-length tap cars in January 1953.

The *Afternoon Hiawatha* withstood Interstate highways and jets to a far better degree than did most other railroads' medium-distance trains. It was a quality conveyance with full diner, Super Dome, and Skytop parlor right to the end on January 21, 1970. Almost the same can be said for the *Morning Hiawatha*, which lasted until Amtrak Day, May 1, 1971, though the *Morning Hi* used a cafeteria diner after 1966, and regular parlor cars replaced the Skytops for about the last year.

NORTH WOODS SERVICE

Throughout its existence, the *Afternoon Hiawatha* connected with daytime trains on the New Lisbon-Wausau-Star Lake line. In June 1936, weekday branch trains 105 and 106 were transformed into the *North Woods Hiawatha*, trains 200 and 201. Initially, they operated with 4400-series coaches and conventional heavyweight lounge and diner-parlor cars. Ten-Wheeler 10 was streamlined to resemble the Atlantics and used on the *Hiawatha — North Woods Section*, as 200 and 201 were first identified. The next year both equipment and motive power were spruced up as the trains acquired a Beaver Tail and tap-diner from the now-surplus original *Hi* trainset. A second shrouded 4-6-0, No. 11, meant that the engine used north of Wausau also appeared modern to the public. The trains ran year round between New Lisbon and Minocqua; during the summer they were extended through the resort area to Star Lake until that line segment was abandoned in 1944. Beginning in 1939 the *North Woods* was operated as an independent mainline

train in the summer and during holiday periods between New Lisbon and Chicago (except in 1943). From 1951 on, Chicago operation was limited to weekends.

In December 1940 the *North Woods*' Beaver Tail and tap-diner were sent to the new *Midwest Hi*. The *North Woods* then used heavyweight parlor-diners until 1949, when the Beaver Tail and the tap-diner returned for two seasons. In 1951 a streamlined *Grove*-series car was assigned to the train.

In April 1943, Pacifics of class F4 displaced the Ten-Wheelers, by then 43 years old. In early 1947, shrouded 4-6-2s 801 and 812 arrived from the Manilla-Sioux Falls line. Their tenure was short — Alco RSC-2 road-switchers replaced them in April 1947.

For a few months early in 1951, Wausau became the northern terminal of the *North Woods*, then service resumed to Woodruff. In April 1956, the trains became a coach-only Wausau-New Lisbon round trip and their *Hiawatha* title was quietly dropped. As 202 and 203, the little locals took down their markers for the last time October 7, 1970.

THE MIDWEST HIAWATHA

It was the Milwaukee Road, whose route missed major intermediate cities, that first established a decent streamliner-era schedule in both directions between Chicago and Omaha — with the *Midwest Hiawatha* December 11, 1940*. Entrusted to the capable class A 4-4-2s, trains 102 and 103 consisted

---

* The starting date of the *Midwest Hiawatha* is shown as December 7 in THE HIAWATHA STORY. The author, who knew better, blushes.

The *Morning Hi* is shown along the Mississippi River between La Crosse and Winona in 1950 behind new FP7s and an F7B. Train 5 usually carried seven or eight express, mail storage, and RPO cars and a like number of passenger cars. — *Milwaukee Road.*

In 1947 the Valley became one of the first two districts of the Milwaukee Road to be dieselized, with all road assignments handled by Alco RSC-2 road-switchers. Number 989 is shown leaving Tomahawk with *Hi* 200 in June 1950. Behind the burbling Alco is RPO-express car 1205, the only one of its type, permanently assigned to the *North Woods Hi*. — *Stanley H. Mailer.*

Train 200 is shown ready to leave Wausau, Wisconsin, January 3, 1937, behind streamlined Ten-Wheeler No. 10. Two 4400-series coaches are between the conventional RPO-express car and the parlor-diner. About three hours ahead the train will meet both Hiawathas at New Lisbon. — *Milwaukee Road.*

On December 11, 1940, Sandra Bock, 8-year-old granddaughter of General Agent W. E. Bock, is about to christen the first departure of the *Midwest Hiawatha* from Omaha. Note the microphone attached to the coupler door to broadcast the sound of the smashing bottle. Shortly train 102 will highball on its dash to Chicago, running most of the distance at nearly 90 miles per hour and making the Burlington, the Rock Island, and the Chicago & North Western sit up and take notice. — *Milwaukee Road: Lucas Photographs.*

Midwest Hiawatha 103 is inspected at speed by three railroaders at Kirkland, Illinois, in July 1943. — *Milwaukee Road.*

Milwaukee competed for passenger traffic to and from Des Moines by operating connecting trains over a 28-mile branch from Madrid, Iowa. Train 200 is shown heading back to Des Moines from Madrid, having delivered Chicago passengers to the *Midwest Hi* and received passengers from Sioux City and Omaha. Atlantic No. 27 reminds us that the larger *Hiawatha* 4-4-2s were a revival of a turn-of-the-century wheel arrangement. Motor cars replaced the steam train in the spring of 1942. — *Verne Philips.*

Dubuque had a connection to the *Midwest Hiawatha* at Green Island. The train's power, 4-4-0 No. 34, built by Rogers in 1904, was replaced by a motor car in early 1942. — *Keith D. Pregler.*

The *Midwest Hiawatha*, train 103, rolls off the Mississippi River bridge into Sabula, Iowa, behind Erie-built 21. The last two Erie-builts the Milwaukee Road purchased lacked the fluted nose trim of the *Olympian* units and were assigned to general service. Bringing up the rear is one of the Kuhler-styled Beaver Tails built in 1938. — *Both photos, Milwaukee Road.*

of Beaver Tail (Chicago-Sioux Falls), straight parlor (Chicago-Omaha), tap-diner, coaches, and mail and express cars, most of the 1937 style.

A double-destination train, the *Midwest Hi* divided at Manilla, in western Iowa, to serve Sioux City and Sioux Falls as trains 132 and 133. Train 132 connected with train 2 from Rapid City to create a journey eight hours faster than previously from the Black Hills to Chicago. Until passenger business began to decline, the *Midwest Hi* had branch line connections, steam or motor trains to Des Moines and Dubuque.

The Sioux Falls section was first powered by gaudily painted F5 Pacifics, then by a pair of 4-6-2s shrouded and painted in the style of the F7 Hudsons. Dieselization of the Midwest occurred in 1946, though occasional trips ran behind the 4-4-2s until at least September 1947.

The 1942 passenger car program included rebuilding the 1937 express-tap cars into mid-train tap-diners for the *Midwest Hi*, simplifying switching at Manilla. In 1948 the *Midwest* received new RPO-express cars, coaches, parlor cars, and tap-diners, and 1938 Beaver Tails.

On October 30, 1955, Milwaukee Road commenced handling Union Pacific's *City* streamliners between Chicago and Council Bluffs, Iowa. The *Midwest Hiawatha* became simply two Sioux Falls coaches attached to the rear of the *Challenger*, trains 107 and 108, plus a tap-diner north of Manilla. Six months later, on April 28, 1956, Union Pacific combined the *Challenger* with the *City of Los Angeles*, bringing an end to the *Midwest Hiawatha* and daytime passenger schedules on Milwaukee's Chicago-Omaha route.

THE OLYMPIAN HIAWATHA

The *Olympian Hiawatha* claimed a number of distinctions. It was the sole member of the tribe to include sleeping cars, it had — though not for long — a unique color scheme, it was the continent's fastest open-platform observation car ride, and it was one of the few trains anywhere to regularly operate with diesel, electric, and steam motive power in the course of a single journey.

Successor to the *Olympian*, it was given the same train numbers, 15 and 16. It entered service June 29, 1947, on a 45-hour timing between Chicago and Seattle, two nights out compared to the *Olympian's* three.

Between Chicago and Minneapolis it was pulled by two-unit E7s. Between Minneapolis and Tacoma, Fairbanks-Morse Erie-builts shattered tradition by operating through both electric zones. These three-unit 6000 h.p. engines brought to CMStP&P its most vibrant diesel color scheme, cresting the train's orange, maroon, and gray with fluted stainless steel nose panels. The cars constructed by Milwaukee Shops in 1947 for this longest-distance *Hi* emerged

with a special livery in which the maroon center panel ran only through the window area. The portions of the cars near the ends were entirely orange below the letter band.

The *Olympian Hiawatha* was hurried into service for 1947's summer travel peak with a mixed consist: new RPO-express, baggage-dormitory, coach, Touralux, tap-cafe, and dining cars and conventional section-bedroom and compartment-drawing room-open platform observation cars from its predecessor. The Touralux cars were intermediate or tourist class open-section sleeping cars. Milwaukee, alone among Western railroads, retained tourist class sleepers. Other western roads dropped them as postwar streamlined equipment was delivered.

Equipment changes began during the first year. The combined Touralux-coach for women and children and the RPO-express car were removed. This made a ten-car consist which could be handled by 4000 h.p. diesels for the entire trip. The F-Ms were regrouped into two-unit machines and used for the full Lake Michigan-Puget Sound run.

About Thanksgiving 1948 the long-awaited all-room sleeping cars began arriving from Pullman-Standard. *Lake*-series cars contained ten roomettes and six bedrooms, while *Creek* cars had eight bedrooms and a Skytop Lounge. The Milwaukee Road insisted upon its own unique solarium design, and the cars were heralded as the "finishing touch to a perfect train." The *Olympian Hi* was fully streamlined by mid-January 1949.

A coal miners' strike in late 1949 saw 15 and 16 become electrified with Westinghouse motors on the Rocky Mountain Division and bipolars on the Coast Division. The Erie-builts were thus able to handle the *Columbian* as well, hastening the retirement of the F6a Hudsons. However, all four trains, 15, 16, 17, and 18, were pulled across the non-electrified gap between Avery, Idaho, and Othello, Washington, by oil-burning 4-6-4s and 4-8-4s. About three years later, new FP7 diesels displaced the Hudsons and Northerns on the Idaho division.

Even in that diesel age, electric traction progressed. Two of the Little Joe 5110 h.p. motors were assigned to the *Hi* and, occasionally, the *Columbian* for six years. Then E22 and E23, members of the original boxcab class of 1915, which had been rebuilt for passenger service, were assigned to 15 and 16 over the Cascades, and the bipolars moved to the Rocky Mountain Division, letting the Joes transfer to freight service.

Santa Claus left Super Domes under the Christmas tree for 15 and 16 in 1952. February 1957 saw the combination of the *Olympian Hiawatha* with the *Afternoon Hiawatha* (train 3 from Chicago to Minneapolis) and with the *Morning Hi* (train 6 from Minneapolis to Chicago). The big trains, which were numbered 15 and 16, used engines from the Chicago-Twin Cities pool.

Train 16, the eastbound *Olympian Hiawatha*, has backed into the station at Butte, Montana. On the rear are two heavyweight Pullmans, for this is the summer of 1948. Eight years later a new station on the road's main line replaced this towered building, which became radio and TV station KXLF. — *Milwaukee Road: Don E. Wolter.*

 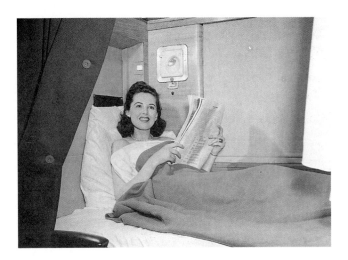 

(Above, left) For a brief season the *Olympian Hiawatha* carried a combination coach and Touralux sleeper for women and children. There was little demand for such segregated facilities, and the cars were withdrawn during the first year of streamlined operation. (Above, center) This pretty passenger is ensconced in a Touralux lower berth. Visible behind her is the niche from which half the bed folded down; the other half folded down from the opposite seat back. Heavy curtains were buttoned to provide privacy when advertising photos weren't being taken. Despite the intermediate fares and low accommodation charges of the Touralux cars, passengers preferred fully enclosed private rooms to Touralux berths — though Touralux cars outlasted the *Olympian Hiawatha*. (Above, right) The outer end of the tavern room of the *Olympian Hi*'s tap-cafe car had curved sofas and modernistic wood-veneer walls; at the other end of the tavern room was an attractive bar. The opposite end of the car contained a coffee shop, and a kitchen separated the two rooms. — *Milwaukee Road.*

The Pullman double bedroom was a marvel of efficient use of space — indeed, all Pullman accommodations were. This is a crosswise room with its window at the foot of the beds and the corridor at the head. The back of the full-width sofa was lowered to become the lower bed; the upper bed was lowered from the ceiling. Lengthwise bedrooms had berths parallel to the rails; by day they had two large armchairs. The toilet and the washbowl were in a fully enclosed annex. Folding walls between pairs of double bedrooms could be opened, as shown here, to create a bedroom suite. — *Milwaukee Road.*

West of Minneapolis the usual lash-up was an E9 and an FP7. In fall 1958 the electric passenger locomotives were withdrawn and the *Olympian Hi* was entirely diesel-powered for its final years.

For one year — from the fall of 1957 to the fall of 1958 — train 16 made the world's fastest start-to-stop run: Tomah to Portage, Wis., averaging 82.5 mph. By 1958 air travel and better competing rail service were taking their toll on patronage of 15 and 16. To counter competition, the road engaged in one of the more innovative passenger promotions of the declining years of privately run rail passenger service. However, the heroics failed, and CMStP&P went before the Interstate Commerce Commission in December 1960 with a plea to discontinue the remaining passenger service west of Minneapolis. On May 22, 1961, the last *Olympian Hiawathas* departed from Chicago and Tacoma.

However, the ICC required that a train with food service and a sleeper be operated between Minneapolis and Butte, Montana. Nameless trains 15 and 16 began operating over that line segment on May 23, 1961, with a leg-rest coach, a Touralux sleeper, and a food service car, which the timetable indicated as a tap-grill but which was often a Super Dome. The train ran essentially on the *Olympian Hi's* schedule, with time added at Butte to turn train 15 before continuing to Deer Lodge, where there was no way to turn the train for its return trip. The trains continued until January 31, 1964, when the service was cut back to Aberdeen, South Dakota.

Coach-only trains 15 and 16 ran for 5 years between Minneapolis and Aberdeen, with a creditable schedule covering 290 miles in 295 minutes, including intermediate stops. They were discontinued on April 16, 1969.

THE CHIPPEWA

The *Chippewa*, a member of the *Hiawatha* tribe between 1948 and 1957, was a train that seized the initiative from a competitor much as the road had with its *Midwest Hiawatha*.

Named for the Indian tribe which once inhabited much of the area they served, trains 14 and 21 entered the Chicago-Green Bay-Iron Mountain, Michigan, market in time for the 1937 Memorial Day weekend. Initially, the *Chip* carried two 4400-series coaches, and standard RPO-express, diner, and parlor. The fall 1938 equipment program transferred the original Beaver Tail parlors from the *North Woods Hi* to 21 and 14, which carried them until the postwar *Hiawatha* expansion.

Within a few months the train was extended north to Channing, a division point; then, from March 1938 until the end of 1953, to Ontonagon on Lake Superior's shore. At various times the *Chip* originated in Milwaukee (receiv-

It's summer 1950 at Milwaukee. Alco diesel No. 14 has arrived from Chicago with train 21, the *Chippewa-Hiawatha*, and will move out of the way so streamlined Pacific 151 can replace it. Atlantic No. 2 stands ready to leave with train 29 for Madison, Wisconsin. In about 20 minutes the westbound *Afternoon Hi* will pause between the two trains, then depart for Minneapolis, followed by the *Chip* and train 29. — *Kalmbach Publishing Co.: Wallace W. Abbey.*

ing Chicago passengers from *Hi* 101), and during part of the 1950s the Channing-Ontonagon portion of the schedule was covered by a motor car.

Class A Atlantics and streamlined and conventional Hudsons took 14 and 21 across the fast Chicago & Milwaukee subdivision. North of Milwaukee, class A 4-4-2s worked briefly to Green Bay, until they were found too heavy for the track. Then F3 Pacifics, at first brightly painted, then in 1941 shrouded 4-6-4 style, handled the train. Occasionally in the late 1940s a conventional F6 Hudson would run as far north as Green Bay (the track had been improved by then). The *Chip* was dieselized in December 1950 with Fairbanks-Morse Erie-builts bumped from main line *Hiawathas* by new FP7s. Later E7s, FP7s, and yellow-painted GP9s took their turns.

Michigan's isolated upper peninsula provided interesting interline connections. At Sidnaw, the Milwaukee Road met the Duluth, South Shore & Atlantic. The two roads agreed to let Train 21 and South Shore 7 to Duluth wait for each other's passengers. The Copper Range Railroad re-entered interline passenger business from June 1944 to November 1946 with a McKeever-Houghton connection, also named *Chippewa* and numbered 14 and 21.

In the summer of 1948 new RPO-express cars, coaches, and dining cars and 1938 Beaver Tails came to 14 and 21 and with them the title *Chippewa-Hiawatha*. This was the train's zenith.

Early in 1951 Chicago-Green Bay locals 10 and 19 were discontinued, and several of their station stops were added to the *Chip*'s schedule. That fall, a *Grove* parlor-diner replaced the Beaver Tail and the full diner. October 1956 saw first-class seating discontinued and full meals replaced by a vending machine coach. Four months later train 14 was discontinued south of Milwaukee, and the coach from the north was attached to Minneapolis-Chicago local train 58. Trains 14 and 21 were now essentially Milwaukee-Channing locals, and the *Hiawatha* portion of their name was dropped. Train 21 made its last trip north on February 1, 1960, and when the markers were taken down on 14 the next evening in Milwaukee, the *Chippewa* era came to an end.

Minneapolis-Aberdeen, South Dakota, train 15, the last remnant of the *Olympian Hiawatha* and the road's last passenger run west of the Twin Cities, awaits departure from Minneapolis in this 1968 scene. — *Don L. Hofsommer.*

The *Chippewa* emerges from Chicago Union Station to cross Canal Street in a 1940s scene. Atlantic No. 1 and the express car will be exchanged at Milwaukee for a smaller shrouded Pacific and an RPO-express car. The *Chip* carried a conventional diner until it became a *Hiawatha* in 1948. — *Milwaukee Road.*

34

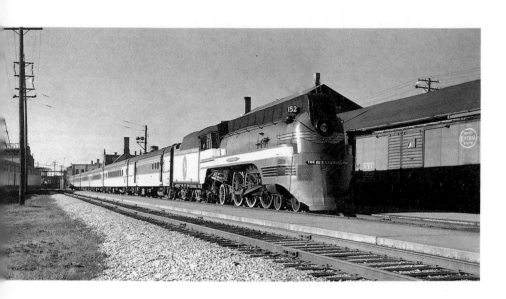

Train 14, the southbound *Chippewa-Hiawatha*, stands in the stub-end station at Washington Avenue in downtown Green Bay in the fall of 1948, shortly after it received new coaches and diner, a Beaver Tail parlor car, and full *Hiawatha* status. — *Brad Kniskern.*

The spring of 1949 has only grudgingly arrived in Green Bay — the snow has melted but the Fox River is still frozen. The *Chippewa-Hiawatha* has posed for company photographers at its streamlined best. Behind the Kuhler-styled Pacific are an RPO-express car and three coaches whose window stripes disclose their original assignment on the *Olympian Hiawatha*, a 1948-built diner, and a 1938 Beaver Tail parlor car. Green Bay Jct. is the switch to the spur to the Washington Avenue station in Green Bay's business district. Train 21 has just backed off that spur and will now pull forward to cross the Fox River to the Oakland Avenue station, designated in the division timetable as Green Bay Shops, then continue north to Michigan's upper peninsula. — *Milwaukee Road.*

OTHER NAME TRAINS OF THE MILWAUKEE ROAD

In the early days of railroading, most passenger trains stopped at all but the most obscure stations — most trains were locals. Until the turn of the century even the slowest train was faster than the alternate means of transportation, horse and buggy on an unpaved road. Most improvements in train travel in that era were in sleeping, dining, and parlor car service, not in speed.

The Milwaukee Road had trains of varying statures on its main line from Chicago through Milwaukee to the Twin Cities. They provided parlor, sleeping, and dining cars as such luxuries were developed within the rail industry. Other Chicago, Milwaukee & St. Paul main lines hosted trains which could be termed prestigious, considering the track structure and density of population in the 1890s. As varnish on the passenger cars was replaced by orange paint and 4-4-0s gave way to Ten-Wheelers and Atlantics, CM&StP had to upgrade its passenger service to better reflect the maturity of its railroad.

First came "limited" trains on important routes; then improvements to cars and motive power. In 1934 came an industry-leading innovation: the Milwaukee Road introduced full-size deluxe streamlined coaches designed and built at the road's Milwaukee, Wisconsin, shops. These tradition-shattering coaches were assigned to the road's prestige trains: the *Arrow, Copper Country Limited, Day Express, Olympian, Pioneer Limited, Sioux,* and *Southwest Limited.* They also entered service on Chicago-Milwaukee and Chicago-Madison, Wis., trains, and train 56, the eastbound *Fast Mail,*

where they were outranked by Railway Post Office and Railway Express cars.

Milwaukee Road encompassed nearly all aspects of the passenger spectrum. Some of its branch line trains were almost shortline in nature: a Ten-Wheeler, an RPO-express, and a single coach. With few exceptions even they could boast of air-conditioning by 1940. A few trains actually ran as mixed trains though were not specified as such in the public timetables. Such arrangements provided time freight service along a branch, leaving local duties for patrols (way freights) running two or three days a week.

SLEEPING CAR SERVICE

With construction of the bridge over the Mississippi River at La Crosse, Wisconsin, in 1876, the railway could fully justify its name: Chicago, Milwaukee & St. Paul. The first through trains between Chicago and the Twin Cities required between 17½ and 20 hours for the journey, so sleeping accommodations were necessary. The CM&StP touted its own sleeping cars, equipped with iron safes for wallets and other valuables, and emphasized its route via Milwaukee. The early sleepers and diners were built by Harlan & Hollingsworth of Wilmington, Delaware.

CM&StP sleepers were the first to run north of Chicago, the first with air brakes, and the first away from the East Coast to be electrically lighted. In

37

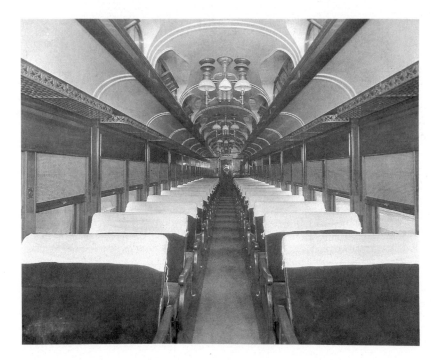

The *Pioneer Limited* of 1927 poses near Pacific Junction in Chicago. (Above) Sleeper-observation car *Minnehaha* brings up the rear. Near the center of the train are one of the upgraded 1908 Barney & Smith lounges and the diner and parlor car the train carried between Chicago and Milwaukee. (Opposite page) Behind the express car is a single coach; 12 first-class cars follow. — *Both photos, Milwaukee Road.*

The limited trains of the 1920s and 1930s were not always as luxurious as they have been described, at least for coach passengers. Coaches like this were used on the Milwaukee's premier *Pioneer Limited* as late as 1927. Though the road was an early user of steam heat and electric lighting, the stove at the far end of the car and the oil lamps overhead indicate a lack of trust in the more modern technology. — *Milwaukee Road.*

September 1888, electric lighting was introduced on trains 1 and 4 between Chicago and the Twin Cities, and six months later the innovation spread to trains 1 and 4 between Chicago and Omaha. Only the Pennsylvania Railroad and the predecessor of the Atlantic Coast Line had electric lights earlier.

Locomotive steam heating of passenger cars was introduced on a trial basis on CM&StP in fall 1887, and in 1892 the road embarked upon a full-scale program to extend such heating to all passenger cars.

Between 1882 and 1890, CM&StP let the Pullman Company operate its sleeping car service, but the railway resumed full control until 1927, when Pullman again entered the picture to operate cars assigned to the *Arrow*, *Olympian*, and *Pioneer Limited*.

Most Milwaukee Road overnight trains were affected by an order of the Office of Defense Transportation on July 15, 1945. To facilitate movement of servicemen, all sleeping cars in the United States were removed from runs of 450 miles or less. Only the *Olympian* and the *Southwest Limited* went completely unscathed. The *Arrow* and the *Sioux* retained cars operating between their end points, but lost sleepers set out at intermediate stations, while the *Copper Country Limited* kept only the Sault Ste. Marie and Calumet cars operated jointly with Soo Line and Duluth, South Shore & Atlantic. The famed *Pioneer Limited* substituted parlor cars. The order was rescinded seven months later.

Pullman slowly extended its scope until, in post-World War Two days, virtually all sleeping cars on the Milwaukee Road were Pullmans. Then, near the end of railroad-operated passenger service, the Pullman Company ceased to exist and the remaining sleeping cars were operated once again by the Milwaukee Road.

Let's look at Milwaukee Road's best-known sleeping-car trains of the steam era: *Pioneer Limited, Copper Country Limited, Southwest Limited, Olympian, Fisherman's Special, Sioux,* and *Arrow.*

THE PIONEER LIMITED

Pioneer Limited was bestowed as a title on trains 1 and 4 in May 1898 in recognition of their being the first through trains between Chicago and Minneapolis. Advertised as solid vestibule trains, they featured a buffet-smoker and all-compartment and section sleepers. The train also carried Milwaukee-Minneapolis sleepers and a Chicago-Milwaukee dining car that served dinner on train 1 and breakfast on train 4. Steward Dan Healey presided over the diner from 1899 until his death in 1922.

In the early 1900s Pullman-built cars entered service with "Pioneer Limited" on their letterboards. Cars *Onalaska* and *Ontonagon* had an innovative floor plan with drawing rooms at the center of the car; earlier cars (and most

The 1927 equipment for the *Pioneer Limited* and the *Olympian* had Timken roller bearings, which not only enhanced the riding quality of the cars but improved safety by virtually eliminating hot boxes, overheated friction bearings. — *Milwaukee Road.*

later ones) had their drawing rooms located at the ends, over the trucks.

At first, the *Pioneer* included reclining-seat coaches, but they later gave way to straight seats as the emphasis shifted to sleeping car comfort. By 1914, 1 and 4 had been gradually re-equipped with steel cars (by then the train name had disappeared from the letterboards), and operation in two sections became the norm until at least 1920.

In 1921 dining car service was added between La Crosse and Minneapolis. By 1923, running times for the *Pioneer Limited* had been reduced by 90 minutes from the original 14 hours. That year, there was a nice feature for women: two 12-section, 1-drawing-room cars on each train had their drawing room replaced with a ladies lounge.

In May 1927, 18 new Pullmans were delivered in 14-section; 12-section, 1-drawing-room; 6-compartment, 3-drawing-room; and 6-single-bedroom, lounge, observation configurations. The last mentioned were the first sleeping cars built with private rooms for one person. To accompany the new Pull-

mans, the Milwaukee Road upgraded existing club and dining cars. One diner was named *Dan Healey* to honor the late steward; it had a further distinction of introducing electric refrigeration to U. S. railroading. All the cars had roller bearings, an innovation which quickly spread to the *Olympian*, the *Arrow*, and other Milwaukee Road trains.

On July 2, 1928, CMStP&P scheduled 1 and 4 to run regularly in two sections. Pullman assigned sleeping cars identical to those built in 1927. West Milwaukee Shops, under the supervision of Karl Nystrom, redecorated the interiors of two club cars in a style approaching art deco. The pair, renamed *Hennepin* and *Ramsey*, had interiors of Bordeaux blue and silver, tables and desks of birdseye maple, and lighting fixtures of old silver. The two-section operation was the only such regular movement on any railroad west of Chicago and was a strong indication of the *Pioneer*'s popularity, but it was made unnecessary in 1930 by powerful new 4-6-4s, the F6 class.

Train 4, which made fewer stops, was down to a running time just under 11 hours by 1931, but not until July 1935 did train 1 match it — and by then train 4 was hurrying along in 8½ hours. Then, spurred on by the *Hiawatha*, the F6s got up on their 79-inch drivers and clipped another 75 minutes from the schedule of train 1 in the fall of 1935, giving the train a Chicago departure time of 10:15 p.m. and a Minneapolis arrival of 8 a.m.

Train 1's later departure eliminated the need for a diner from Chicago to Milwaukee, but the train picked up a cafe-observation car at La Crosse to serve breakfast. (The car returned to La Crosse from Minneapolis on train 56, the *Fast Mail*.) Replacement of the Pullman open-platform observation car with a double-bedroom solarium Pullman facilitated adding the cafe-observation car at La Crosse.

In December 1940, a 14-single-bedroom car was added to the Pioneer. In August 1942, the club car was discontinued in favor of a buffet-diner operating the entire distance on both trains, offering evening lounge and morning breakfast service.

Streamlined coaches were added to the *Pioneer* in 1934, and each re-equipping of the *Twin Cities Hiawathas* resulted in the replaced coaches being cascaded to the *Pioneer*. E7 diesels replaced steam on the *Pioneer* in mid-1946, though occasional 4-6-4 runs were made even after 1948. In 1948 the train acquired brand-new streamlined coaches, tap-diner, baggage-dormitory, and sleeping cars.

At times full diners replaced the tap-diners; at other times *Grove*-series parlor-diners, reconfigured to diner-lounges, were assigned to the train. Sleeping cars were generally of the duplex-roomette types. When the *Pioneer* made its final departures on September 7, 1970, it carried but a single sleeper plus a diner-lounge and coaches.

Class H6 4-4-0 No. 726 was built for the Milwaukee & Northern and is shown in home territory at Lena, Wisconsin, sometime after its 1899 renumbering. — *Milwaukee Road.*

THE COPPER COUNTRY LIMITED

By 1899, an interline service was in place between Chicago and Calumet, Michigan, operated by the CM&StP south of Champion, Mich., and by the Duluth, South Shore & Atlantic north of there. The *Copper Country Limited* name seems to have been used first in a March 1907 timetable ad, when 2 and 3 were apparently considered to be on a par with CM&StP's *Pioneer Limited* and *Southwest Limited*. Their schedule endured for many years, offering a late-evening departure from Chicago with a noontime arrival in the copper country and a late afternoon departure from Calumet with breakfast-time arrival in Chicago.

Trains 2 and 3 had electric lights, an uncommon luxury at the time, especially in remote areas such as the upper peninsula of Michigan. The trains carried a Milwaukee-Marquette, Mich., sleeper, which was interchanged with the South Shore at Republic, Mich., 10 miles south of Champion. A dining car served breakfast north out of Iron Mountain, Mich., and dinner south from Champion. For a while the car ran as far south as Ellis Junction (now Crivitz), Wis. From 1909 to 1928, the South Shore provided the diner, which operated as far north as Summit, Mich., south of L'Anse on the DSS&A. Between 1910 and 1920, approximately, sleepers also operated between Chicago and Calumet via McKeever, Mich., and the Copper Range

Pictured on the Copper Range Railroad but running with Milwaukee Road locomotive, cars, and crew, is train 103, the *Copper Range Limited*, a contemporary of the *Copper Country Limited*. The train was renamed the *Northern Michigan Special* in 1913, three years after this photo was taken. Ten-Wheeler 202 was built by Milwaukee Shops in 1906. Copper Range crews and locomotives handled the train between Houghton and Calumet, Michigan. — *Milwaukee Road.*

Railroad, on a route 25 miles longer but with approximately the same running time. This service evolved into the *Northern Michigan Special*, which ran until 1923.

During the 1920s the number of sleeping cars on the *Copper Country* varied. In addition to those to Calumet, railroad-owned sleepers operated at one time or another to Champion and Menominee, Mich. The Menominee car, which bounced over the branch east from Ellis Junction, was subsequently given Iron Mountain as its northern terminal, and still later ran between Chicago and Green Bay.

In September 1930 a major change occurred in the northbound schedule.

In the summer of 1948 the *Southwest Limited* was dieselized with a pair of Fairbanks-Morse Erie-builts like those assigned to the *Olympian Hi*, except for the omission of the fluted trim on the nose. Train 25 is shown on the wye track at Sturtevant, Wisconsin, in July 1949. Visible behind the diesel are a conventional express car, prewar streamlined express car, a 1947 RPO-express, a modernized conventional coach, a 1934 *Hiawatha* coach, and a Milwaukee Road sleeper for Omaha. Behind the orange sleeper are a Pullman for Kansas City and a diner lounge. — W. H. N. Rossiter.

The *Copper Country Limited* was renumbered 9 and departed four hours earlier, replacing, in part, a Chicago-Green Bay train. The *Copper Country Limited* carried dining cars in both directions between Chicago and Green Bay and between Channing and Calumet, plus a parlor car from Chicago to Green Bay, a Calumet sleeper, and a Sault Ste. Marie sleeper which had been established that June via Soo Line east of Pembine, Wis.

Train 3 remained in the timetable, becoming the *Iron Country Limited* to Iron River, Mich., via the branch from Kelso Junction. The *Iron Country*'s Iron River, Channing, and Green Bay sleepers returned on train 2 because Train 3 had no southbound counterpart. (Instead there was a daytime local which later became the *Chippewa*.)

The Depression took its toll in equipment and schedules. Train 2 terminated at Milwaukee, and its through coaches and sleepers were forwarded to Chicago on train 4, the *Pioneer Limited*, an arrangement that lasted off and on into the diesel era. In July 1936, air-conditioned sleepers were assigned to the *Copper Country Limited*. Two years later dining car service was eliminated north of Milwaukee, but the train schedules were appreciably quickened when local stops between Milwaukee and Green Bay were transferred to a new pair of daytime locals. At the same time, the *Iron Country Limited* was discontinued and its northbound sleeping cars returned to the *Copper Country*.

In the fall of 1939 the Calumet sleeper became a Pullman car, while the Sault Ste. Marie and Iron River cars remained Milwaukee Road-operated. A few months later train 709 from Channing to Iron River began to handle freight cars, making it one of the few routes in the United States where first-class travelers could partake of mixed train service. The Iron River car deadheaded back to Channing on the mixed train, then ran from there to Chicago on train 2. The sleeper on the Iron River mixed train was discontinued in the spring of 1949. Diesel power was introduced early in 1952, accelerating the *Copper Country Limited* in both directions.

The frequency of the Sault Ste. Marie sleeper was reduced several times in the 1950s: to six nights a week in 1954, and to three nights a week and soon afterward to two nights a week in 1956. It was discontinued entirely after the 1958 summer season, and the Soo Line train which had carried the Chicago-Sault Ste. Marie car north of Pembine was discontinued in 1960.

In October 1955 train 2 was renumbered 10, as part of the systemwide renumbering of trains prompted by the operation of Union Pacific's *City* streamliners between Chicago and Council Bluffs. By 1960 the train carried but a single sleeper, a 6-roomette, 8-duplex-roomette, 4-double-bedroom car between Chicago and Calumet. It became triweekly in the spring of 1964.

Many secondary trains were kept alive by mail service. In the 1960s the Post Office began a wholesale conversion from sorting mail in transit to sectional sorting centers. The discontinuance of a Railway Post Office usually meant the discontinuance of a passenger train soon afterward. The *Copper Country Limited* lost its RPO in October 1967 and made its last departures on March 7, 1968.

THE SOUTHWEST LIMITED

The *Southwest Limited* was placed in operation between Chicago and Kansas City, Missouri, on December 6, 1903, in celebration of the opening of CM&StP's Kansas City cutoff from Ashdale, Illinois, east of Savanna, through Davenport to Rutledge, Iowa. The new train was accorded status equal to that of the *Pioneer Limited*. The 4-4-2 in charge of the train headed a consist of two or three baggage cars, a coach, a reclining seat coach, a diner, two sleepers, and a compartment-library-observation car, all electrically illuminated. It ran on a 6 p.m. to 9 a.m. schedule in both directions. Train numbers were 5 and 12.

Initially, on certain dates the train also carried a tourist (economy) sleeping car for Los Angeles which was forwarded by the Missouri Pacific to Pueblo, Colorado, the Denver & Rio Grande to Ogden, Utah, and the Southern Pacific to Los Angeles via Oakland.

When the 4-6-2 became the road's standard locomotive for limiteds in 1910, the *Southwest*'s schedules were tightened. A few years later the trains were renumbered 25 and 26. During most of these years, *Southwest* dining cars ran Chicago-Davis Junction, Ill., and Chillicothe, Mo.-Kansas City.

A significant change in emphasis occurred in March 1926 when a Milwaukee-Davenport, Iowa, section of the *Southwest Limited* was inaugurated. At first, only the sleeping car actually ran Milwaukee-Kansas City. Except for an awkward change for northbound coach patrons at Davenport at 3 a.m., the new train, which also carried the numbers 25 and 26, maintained the high quality of service expected of the *Southwest Limited*. A cafe-observation car ran between Milwaukee and Davenport to serve meals and provide parlor-car seating as needed, and a connecting train ran between Beloit and Madison, Wis. The Wisconsin section of the *Southwest* operated via Savanna, Ill., where it exchanged an Omaha-Milwaukee sleeping car with the *Arrow*. (The Chicago section bypassed Savanna on the Ashdale Cutoff.) An Iowa section of the *Southwest* operated from 1927 to 1936 — a Kansas City-Cedar Rapids sleeping car carried in branchline local trains between Cedar Rapids and Ottumwa. During the Depression, those trains, 125 and 126, were powered by motor cars.

December 8, 1928, was the Southwest's twenty-fifth anniversary, and cake was served in the diner. Sleeping car conductor Kelley and porters Foote and Hall, who had staffed the train since its first trip, helped celebrate.

In the spring of 1931, the *Arrow* and the *Southwest* were combined between Chicago and Savanna for economic reasons, ending use of the Ashdale Cutoff by 25 and 26. Thereafter the *Southwest Limited* was a Milwaukee-Kansas City train with usually no more than a single Chicago-Kansas City sleeping car. For three months during the fall of 1934, when 4400-series streamlined coaches were added to the consist, train 25 ran independently from Chicago to Savanna. During 1934, the observation and dining cars be-

In the mid-1920s the Olympian crossed the Cascades by day. The westbound train is shown descending Snoqualmie Pass behind one of the distinctive bipolars that was practically a trademark of the Milwaukee. — *Milwaukee Road: Asahel Curtis.*

A late-1920s *Olympian* is shown climbing around Adair Loop on its way to the summit of the Bitterroots in northern Idaho. This equipment served, with a few modifications, until the advent of the *Olympian Hiawatha.* — *Milwaukee Road: Asahel Curtis.*

The Rockies were equally scenic. Here a Westinghouse "Quill" leads an *Olympian* of the early 1920s through Sixteen Mile Canyon in Montana. Note the cast emblems that have been applied to the side of the locomotive. — *Milwaukee Road: Asahel Curtis.*

tween Kansas City and Milwaukee were air-conditioned, and by then all but the Cedar Rapids car had become Pullmans — and air-conditioned cars were assigned in 1935. By then meal-service cars no longer ran the entire distance; cafe-observations made Kansas City-Ottumwa and Milwaukee-Savanna round trips.

By summer 1947 class F6 Hudsons replaced the venerable F3 Pacifics between Milwaukee and Kansas City, a change made possible by the opening of the Truman Bridge across the Missouri River in 1945. Fall 1948 saw the end of cafe-observation service between Kansas City and Chillicothe, but a 10-section solarium sleeper was assigned as the Chicago Pullman. At the same time, the *Southwest Limited* was entrusted to single Fairbanks-Morse Erie-built diesels.

In the late 1940s and early 1950s the discontinuance of interstate trains was subject to the whims of state regulatory bodies. If a railroad was fortunate enough to be able to drop a money-losing local train, other trains on that route were usually required to assume their stops and duties to preserve service to the small towns along the route. The resulting slower schedules discouraged long-distance rides and rarely brought any additional local business.

In the fall of 1949 quite a few stops and nearly an hour's running time were added to the *Southwest Limited* when Milwaukee-Freeport local trains 21 and 36 were discontinued. It became faster to travel via Chicago and the Santa Fe's new *Kansas City Chief*. The *Southwest* lost its Milwaukee-Kansas City Pullman by summer 1951 and its Chicago-Kansas City Pullman in January 1955.

The *Southwest Limited* name was dropped October 30, 1955, and on April 25, 1958, the Savanna-Kansas City line became freight-only. The final vestiges of the *Southwest Limited*, Milwaukee-Savanna coach-only local trains 25 and 26, made their last departures October 6, 1965, from Milwaukee, and October 7 from Savanna.

THE OLYMPIAN

The Puget Sound Extension was completed May 14, 1909. During the ensuing two years local passenger service with sleeping and dining cars operated across the new line. May 28, 1911, the Northwest's first all-steel trains, the

In 1929 the eastbound *Columbian*, train 18, crossed northern Idaho during the midmorning. The beauty of the scenery along the St. Joe River was justification enough for an unscheduled stop for the company photographer.
— *Milwaukee Road: Asahel Curtis.*

Olympian and the *Columbian*, entered service over the only railroad running the entire distance between Lake Michigan and Puget Sound. Seven sets of equipment were needed for the *Olympian*. The train required 72 hours for the Chicago-Seattle trip, with additional time to and from Tacoma. Sleeping cars and observation-lounges were constructed by Barney & Smith; Pullman built the tourist sleepers and diners. The observation cars contained a ladies' tea room, men's smoking room, library, and buffet, and offered barber and bath service. Within a couple years, further amenities were added to the observation car: a phone for use in terminals, tailor service, and special "Olympian-grams" containing news and stock market reports. Sleeping cars had adjustable window screens, and the coaches had highback seats. Electric lighting was standard, of course, and all cars were vacuum cleaned daily en route.

Effective September 28, 1913, the Milwaukee (as the public was already calling the railway) began passenger service over its recently constructed Idaho & Western branch between Plummer Junction, Idaho, and Spokane. One pair of trains met the *Olympian*; the other — which met the *Columbian* — continued down a branch from St. Maries, Idaho, to Elk River. The mainline limiteds bypassed Spokane, running via Malden, Wash. (as through freights did until the line was abandoned in 1980), but the next year, thanks to trackage rights over Union Pacific, the *Olympian* and *Columbian* began operating via Spokane.

Olympian consists were relatively stable. In 1920 a Spokane setout sleeper was operated to and from Chicago. The next year, since 15 and 16 were daytime trains across Washington, they acquired a parlor car between Spokane and Tacoma. The famous mountain observation cars were included in the consist during summer months over all scenic sections traversed during daylight. They were used primarily in electrified territory, but occasionally ventured west of Avery, Idaho, over the Idaho division to St. Maries, in oil-fired steam locomotive territory.

Electrification was phased in across the Belt, Rocky, and Bitterroot ranges between Harlowton, Montana, and Avery, Idaho, between 1915 and 1917, and across the Saddles and Cascades between Othello and Tacoma, Wash., in 1920. Until the spur into downtown Seattle was electrified in 1927, the motors laid over at Black River while steam engines equipped with headlight and pilot on the rear of the tender shuttled trains to and from Seattle Union Station.

The first passenger electrics were two-unit boxcabs identical to the first freight motors except for gearing and steam heating boilers. With expansion of electrification to the Coast Division, those units were converted for freight duties, and two distinctive styles of passenger motors came onto the property. General Electric constructed five bipolar engines, and Westinghouse built ten

The Milwaukee provided an exceptionally high degree of comfort and modernity with the streamlined coaches introduced on principal trains in 1934, and it improved catering facilities as well. The dining car kitchen prepared fresh food and coffee, which were sold by a waiter passing through the coaches shortly before dining car meal times. — *Milwaukee Road.*

Despite the Pullman badge on the porter's cap, this is a Milwaukee Road-operated tourist sleeper of the style used on the *Olympian* in the early 1930s. The upper berth, lowered for illustrative purposes, was the daytime storage area for all bedding. The seats below have been pushed together to form the foundation for the lower berth, the mattress for which is still in the upper berth. At night, portable headboards were placed between sections and heavy curtains were hung from the overhead rods for privacy. Access to the upper was by means of a small ladder brought on request by the porter. The porter, whose sleeve stripes indicate 35 years of service, was probably borrowed from a first-class Pullman for the photo. — *Milwaukee Road.*

When Milwaukee's tourist cars were air-conditioned, they received permanent headboards and modernized light fixtures, making them virtually identical with their first-class Pullman cousins. — *Milwaukee Road.*

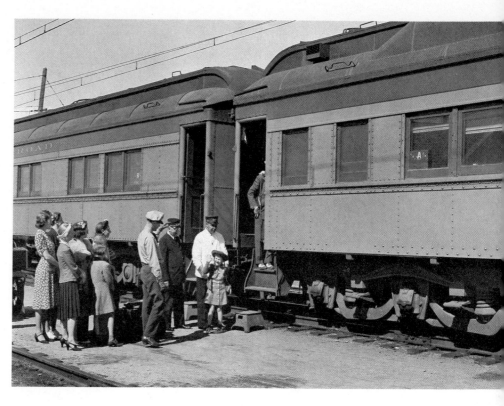

On the second day out of Chicago, the *Olympian* paused at Three Forks, Montana, to change engine crews, restock the diner, and fill the water tanks of the cars. The Milwaukee Road maintained a small dairy there, and passengers were invited to enjoy a cool glass of buttermilk while making the transfer to railroad-operated buses to Gallatin Gateway Inn and Yellowstone National Park. (Above left) On this summer day about 1936, Yellowstone business is good, to judge by the quantity of baggage the driver is wheeling from the first-class cars to his bus. Two sections of train 15 are being operated; this is the sleeper section. The nearest car is the diner; ahead are two tourist sleepers, a 1934 baggage car, and a Westinghouse Quill electric. Behind the diner are, assuredly, more than the usual two Pullmans, full lounge car, and open observation car. — *Milwaukee Road: Torkel Korling.* (Above right) Tourist sleeper conductor and porter watch as a young passenger and a Gallatin Gateway bus driver exchange farewell waves. — *Milwaukee Road.*

long quill-drive boxcabs, which were the only non-GE electrics on the road.

The bipolars became a symbol of the road. They had no gears — their motor armatures were mounted directly on their axles, making them virtually noiseless. But it was their curved hood-center cab styling which drew most attention to the 1-B-D-D-B-1 motors.

The bipolars were big, but the Westinghouse motors, referred to as "quills"

because of their drive system, were even longer and more powerful. Indeed, their weight and length and the difficulty of getting their 2-C-1 + 1-C-2 wheel arrangement around curves created problems. Motor 10301 returned to its builder in the mid-1920s and was cut apart into two 2-C-2 units. The conversion was not successful. About 1928 the severed parts made a second trip east to be restored to their original configuration.

The Gallatin Gateway Inn was opened in 1927 near Salesville, Montana (now Gallatin Gateway), in a bid for a greater share of Yellowstone Park travel. Milwaukee Road's own stretched Fords brought tourists to the inn from the *Olympian* at Three Forks; Yellowstone Park buses operated from the hotel into the park. The inn was sold to a private operator in the early 1950s and closed a few seasons later; it was reopened in 1988. — *Milwaukee Road.*

The frames of the Quills required continual rewelding. By the late 1930s the motors had been designated single-end locomotives, and they received modern striping along their sides and around the front. They were Rocky Mountain Division engines — rarely did they appear on the Coast Division.

In August 1927, the *Olympian* was re-equipped, gaining up-to-the-minute Pullman-operated observation lounges and sleepers. The Pullmans had Spanish-style interiors, at the time very much in vogue. All berths had coil spring mattresses. The running time of the *Olympian* had been reduced to 70 hours in September 1924, and was brought down to 68 hours between Chicago and Seattle a year after the new cars arrived.

Summer 1929 brought a significant speed-up, five hours faster westbound and seven hours faster eastbound. Train 15 departed from Chicago two hours earlier at 9 p.m. but arrived in Seattle at 10 a.m. instead of late afternoon. Number 16 left Seattle in the early evening to arrive in Chicago shortly after breakfast. Two years later, nearly four hours more was taken from the schedules in both directions, reflecting that the new 4-6-4 locomotives had proven themselves east of Harlowton. Until the advent of the Hudsons, class F3 Pacifics handled trains 15 and 16 between Chicago and Mobridge (with engine changes at Milwaukee, La Crosse, Minneapolis, and Aberdeen), while smaller-drivered, more powerful F5s pulled them between the Missouri River and the Rocky Mountain electric zone. The new 6400 series engines were changed only in Minneapolis.

Tried opposite the Baldwin 4-6-4s was the road's first 4-8-4, No. 9700, basically a stretched F6. It also ran freight trials in the Midwest before going to the Idaho division, where the schedules were such that it could make a daily round trip on the *Olympian*. Prior to its arrival, class F4 4-6-2s and even articulated N3 simple 2-6-6-2s pulled 15 and 16 between the two electrified zones. Running times of the *Olympian* were modified only slightly during subsequent years.

There were occasional changes in car styles and assignments. During some seasons before the Depression, through Pullmans continued on the branch from Three Forks, Mont., right to the Gallatin Gateway Inn, CMStP&P's Yellowstone National Park hotel.

The faster schedule 15 and 16 received in January 1931 served to mitigate the route changes and eventual termination of the *Columbian*, which was re-routed the next month between Chicago and Aberdeen, South Dakota, via Manilla, Iowa, and Mitchell, S. Dak. (eastbound it was combined with the *Pacific Limited* from Manilla to Chicago).

Because the westbound *Olympian* overtook the *Columbian*, they were combined west of Spokane; after the rerouting of 17 and 18 the consolidation took place at Butte, Mont. Replacing 17, at first west of Spokane, then from

The sleeping car section of the *Olympian* follows the valley of the Clark Fork River near Bonner Junction, Montana, a short distance east of Missoula. The westbound train has a heavyweight baggage car, three tourist sleepers, streamlined diner, three first-class Pullmans, and a sleeper-observation. Across the valley is Northern Pacific's main line. — *Milwaukee Road.*

Butte to Seattle, was a new train named the *Washington*. The *Columbian* was withdrawn completely in May 1931, as was the *Washington* west of Spokane. A pair of locals, 7 and 8, was inaugurated to provide overnight service between Butte and Spokane. They disappeared from the timetable during the depths of the Depression but returned to operate until mid-1947.

Air-conditioned club-observation and dining cars were added to the *Olympian*'s consist in time for the 1934 Yellowstone season, and streamlined coaches and coach-dormitory cars (for dining-car crews) joined the train that fall. Improved tourist sleeping cars had been introduced the previous year. The *Olympian* was fully air-conditioned by June 1935.

Two years later, double bedrooms were introduced in an updated Pullman, and new *Hiawatha*-type diners regularly appeared in the consist. A report prepared by an outside firm for the then-bankrupt CMStP&P stated the *Olympian*'s increased attractiveness enabled it to just about break even.

The summer of 1941 marked the final operation of the mountain observation cars, which by then were used only between Harlowton and Avery, since the *Olympian* crossed the Cascades in darkness. To afford greater sleeping capacity, the *City* lounge-observations were replaced by *Crystal-* and *Silver-*series 3-compartment, 2-drawing room, lounge-observations, still with open platforms. By December 1943, 15 and 16 were operating regularly the entire distance in coach and sleeping car sections. Every effort was made, not always successfully, to use only streamlined coaches. This frequently necessitated borrowing such cars from other trains — except the *Hiawathas* and the *Pioneer Limited*. The coach section often was pulled east of Minneapolis by S3 4-8-4s that were delivered in 1944. Larger, heavier class S2 Northerns built in 1938 had been operating between Minneapolis and Harlowton whenever the *Olympian* exceeded 12 cars, and they could maintain the schedule with as many as 20 cars. S1 251 was built at Milwaukee Shops (with Baldwin parts) in 1938 and sent to the Idaho division where it joined its older twin 250 (ex-9700) to pull the *Olympian*.

By May 1947, two-section operation of the *Olympian* had ended, and new Fairbanks-Morse Erie-built three-unit diesels were pulling 15 and 16, even through the electric zones, in anticipation of the June arrival of the *Olympian Hiawatha*.

THE COLUMBIAN

When the *Olympian* became a *Hiawatha* on June 29, 1947, its old schedule continued as the revived *Columbian*, trains 17 and 18, with a consist differing but slightly from that of the train it replaced. Two sleepers, one tourist and one standard Pullman, were removed, and a 10-section observation car replaced the 3-drawing-room, 2-compartment observation cars, which were transferred to the *Olympian Hiawatha*. Butte-Spokane locals 7 and 8 ended their overnight trips two months later. The *Columbian* experienced changes in equipment during the next several months: Only a single tourist sleeper remained; the diners, built in 1937 for the *Olympian*, were changed to diner-lounges by replacing the four tables farthest from the kitchen with ten lounge chairs; and the Chicago-Tacoma Pullman became a 6-section, 6-double-bedroom car.

Motive power changed as well. Class F6 Hudsons continued between Minneapolis and Harlowton until the coal miners' strike of late 1949. The Erie-builts of the *Olympian Hi* ceased operating through the electric zones and began handling the *Columbian* as well east of Harlowton. Oil-burning 4-6-4s and 4-8-4s handled 17 and 18 across the Idaho division; the trains continued to have electric power on the Rocky Mountain and Coast divisions.

Curtailments in equipment continued since passenger trains, particularly those of lower status, were beginning to suffer from air and automobile com-

Rolling into Star Lake, a popular north woods destination in the 1930s, is train 215, the *Tomahawk*. Behind the dual-service Ten-Wheeler are an express car from Chicago, an RPO-express car and a coach from New Lisbon, sleepers from Milwaukee and Chicago, and a diner-lounge-observation from New Lisbon. — *Parfitt photo, collection of Walter Harles.*

petition. Early in 1952 a 10-section, buffet-lounge car replaced a 10-section, 1-compartment, 1-drawing room car as the Spokane-Tacoma Pullman, and it was discontinued as spring turned into summer. In 1953 the diner-lounges were replaced by tap-grill cars made surplus by arrival of the Super Domes. Quick evening dinners at division-point beaneries supplemented the tap-grill's menu. In late September 1953, the *Pioneer Limited* and the *Columbian* were consolidated east of the Twin Cities. Only a coach and a sleeper, the latter a Touralux no longer needed for the *Olympian Hiawatha*, operated to and from Chicago. Thus 17 and 18 became streamliners, if briefly.

In January 1955 the *Columbian* became a coach-only Minneapolis-Avery, Idaho, schedule. March 7 of that year 17 and 18 bowed out west of Marmarth, North Dakota, and the *Columbian* name was quietly dropped. In May 1955 they became Minneapolis-Aberdeen trains. In mid-February 1957 the train was cut back further, to Ortonville, Minnesota, and given a new schedule eastbound, to bring No. 18 into Minneapolis by 5:30 p.m. instead of the traditional late-evening arrival. Trains 17 and 18 were discontinued altogether April 1, 1957.

The westbound *Columbian* arrives at Othello, Washington, east end of the Coast Division electrification, behind homemade 4-8-4 251 in January 1948. — *Wade Stevenson.*

Brand-new GP9s pull train 18, the eastbound *Columbian*, through northern Idaho in the summer of 1954. A conventional sleeper is substituting for the streamlined Touralux car usually carried at the rear of the train. — *Joseph Sweeney.*

53

The final steam-powered passenger train on the Wisconsin Valley line was train 215, the *Tomahawk*, on the morning of April 21, 1947. The train is shown approaching the Chicago & North Western crossing in Wausau. The photographer made advance arrangements with the fireman for the heavy display of smoke. — *David Kuechle*.

THE FISHERMAN'S SPECIAL

Recognizing the budding vacation possibilities of northern Wisconsin, CM&StP during the summers of 1912 and 1913 operated special weekend sleeping car service between Chicago and Star Lake, then the north end of the Wisconsin Valley Division. Friday night's cars ran from Chicago to New Lisbon in train 101, and Monday morning the sleepers arrived in Chicago as part of the *Pioneer Limited*. The trains were listed in the Valley timetable as 41 and 42. From 1914 to 1917, 41 and 42 operated to and from Chicago and included a diner.

Because of the war the train did not operate in 1918, but it resumed in 1919 as the *Fisherman's Special*. In 1923 patronage warranted daily operation, which continued through the 1931 season, although that year the *Fisherman*, as it was renamed in 1930, was appended to the *Pioneer Limited* on the main line. A dining-observation car operated north of Wausau, Wis.

Economic conditions forced a cutback to a Friday night north-Sunday night south schedule for 1932 and 1933, but daily service resumed in 1934. In 1935, the train was again reduced to weekend trips, a schedule prevailing for the remainder of its career. *Fisherman* sleepers became air-conditioned in the 1936 season as did the buffet-diner and coaches the next summer. After the 1942 season the train was suspended for the duration of the war.

During the postwar years, the *Fisherman* was combined with the *Copper Country Limited*, trains 9 and 2, between Chicago and Milwaukee and carried numbers 209 and 202 between Milwaukee and Woodruff, since 1944 the north end of the Valley line. Throughout its career, when operating west of Milwaukee as an independent train, the *Fisherman* usually stopped at Oconomowoc, Portage, and Wisconsin Dells. On the Wisconsin Valley line the *Fisherman* stopped at Wisconsin Rapids, Wausau, Merrill, Tomahawk, and all stations north.

The first postwar departure of train 209 from Milwaukee consisted entirely of heavyweight standard cars: coaches, diner-lounge, and two sleepers. Motive power was a class F3 Pacific. Beyond New Lisbon, hand-fired Ten-Wheelers were the usual power, though diesels may well have handled the train after the dieselization of the Valley in 1947. Summer 1948 was the *Fisherman*'s last season.

THE SIOUX

June 20, 1926, a new train, 11 and 22, entered service between Chicago and Sioux Falls, S. Dak., via Madison, Wis., and northern Iowa. Prior to the

(Right) Alco 978 leads the eastbound *Sioux* near Sioux Falls in July 1950. The train is a good example of a non-*Hiawatha* Milwaukee Road train: streamlined headend cars and coaches and heavyweight sleeper. The RSC-2s were the dominant means of dieselizing the Iowa & Dakota Division west of Sheldon, Iowa, and also the Wisconsin Valley and Sioux City-Mitchell-Aberdeen lines. (Below) Canton, South Dakota, saw a flurry of activity each morning. First, train 2 arrived from Rapid City to connect with the *Midwest Hiawatha* for Chicago. Then two hours later Train 11, the *Sioux*, arrived off the line across northern Iowa and divided into Rapid City and Sioux Falls sections. To the latter section was added the railroad-operated 10 section-drawing room-compartment sleeper and streamlined coach which had arrived from Rapid City. The Sioux Falls section stands ready to depart behind Alco RSC-2 No. 977 on this July 1950 day.
— *Both photos, Henry J. McCord.*

55

By the summer of 1956 the *Sioux* between Mason City, Iowa, and Canton, South Dakota, had become a local carrying a brace of older streamlined coaches and an assortment of headend cars. E7 No. 17B is in charge of train 11 west of Dickens, Iowa. The train will shortly brake for the 15-minute stop at Spencer, long enough for coffee and a quick sandwich at the hotel next to the station. — *Don L. Hofsommer.*

first departure from Chicago, Jerry Welch, CM&StP's assistant secretary-treasurer in New York, was in Chicago, and was shown train 11 by Joseph Caldwell, assistant general passenger agent. Welch asked what the new train was called. Upon being told it had no title, he ventured that since its western terminal was Sioux Falls an appropriate name would be the *Sioux*.

The *Sioux* carried three railway-owned 12-section, 1-drawing-room sleepers, one each to Mason City, the Twin Cities (by connecting trains north of Calmar, Iowa), and Sioux Falls. Cafe-observation cars provided dinner, evening lounge service, and breakfast.

In 1927 the *Sioux* was extended west to Rapid City, S. Dak. It became the second-place mileage champion among the Milwaukee Road's passenger trains — only the Puget Sound runs of the *Olympian* and *Columbian* exceeded 11 and 22's mileage. The Minnesota section of the *Sioux* received a cafe-observation and a sleeper to Jackson, Minn., handled west of Austin on Southern Minnesota Division trains 7 and 6 (later 311 and 322).

After the summer of 1931, train 11 terminated at Sioux Falls, and the westbound Rapid City sleeping car was transferred on another train. The eastbound *Sioux* continued to originate at Rapid City. For a brief period in the early 1930s it carried a sleeper from Madison, Wis., to Chicago.

By June 1934 the *Sioux* had acquired additional stops west of Mason City, but the train's appointments had become more elaborate. A full dining car — the first air-conditioned car on the train — and a full-length observation car were placed in Chicago-Madison service.

During the same period, the Mason City set-out sleeper was transferred to local train 3 from Chicago via Savanna. That car resumed its journey west the next morning on train 11, bound for the Black Hills. The car's eastbound run was almost a straight shot from Rapid City to Chicago on 22 — almost, because by then 11 and 22 were not through trains to and from Rapid City.

The *Sioux* arrives Spencer, Iowa, on a cold day in December 1959 behind an FP7 and an Erie-built B unit. Two RPO-express cars with their mail apartments adjoining cope with the Christmas mail. — *Don L. Hofsommer.*

Train 11 terminated in Mitchell, S. Dak., at noon, and its sleeper and coach continued on train 3 after an eight-hour wait. Train 22 ran from Rapid City to Chicago, but it paused for two hours at Mitchell.

Another unlikely car movement of that era was that of the parlor-solarium which worked afternoon train 23 from Chicago through Milwaukee to Madison, then ran in 11 from Madison through Calmar to Minneapolis, returning to Chicago on mainline local train 58. In some seasons this car was a full lounge, and its Minneapolis-Chicago trip was on train 56, the *Fast Mail*.

Next summer, 1935, the Mason City-Sioux Falls cafe-observation enjoyed air-conditioning, but the Chicago diner was a non-air-conditioned car. Perhaps in compensation, the club car now was extended to Marquette from Madison. Contemporary records indicate CMStP&P did not have as many air-conditioned cars as other roads in its territory, and the *Sioux*'s air-conditioned diner may have been transferred to a train subject to direct competition. The introduction of streamlined coaches may have compensated. However, they did not run west of Mitchell, as if to indicate that the *Sioux* was a Chicago-Mitchell train.

February 2, 1936, saw a significant route change for train 11 — via Milwaukee, with a full diner operating Chicago-Milwaukee. Soon afterward the Chicago-Rapid City sleeper was restored and the parlor-diner from Mason City was routed to Mitchell, relegating Sioux Falls to service by a stub train from Canton. *Sioux* sleepers became air-conditioned.

By summer 1937 the *Sioux* was completely air-conditioned. For about six weeks in August and September, 22 also ran via Milwaukee. Until early 1938, the eastbound Jackson sleeper was routed to a Milwaukee termination via commuter train 12, which was extended west from Watertown to Madison to make the connection.

In early spring 1938 a new train 3, the Chicago-Mason City *Marquette*, was inaugurated. It carried cars for Jackson and Minneapolis — that section of the train was known as the *Minnesota Marquette* — in addition to those for its Mason City terminus. At the same time train 11, the *Sioux*, was reduced to a single sleeper (to Rapid City) and acquired the stops of a discontinued local train between Madison and Marquette, Iowa. Within a year, the *Marquette*'s Jackson sleeping car and the *Sioux*'s Chicago-Madison club car were discontinued.

April 28, 1940, train 11 returned to the Janesville route. With the introduction of the *Midwest Hiawatha* between Sioux Falls and Chicago in December 1940, train service on the line west of Canton, S. Dak., was altered considerably, and the *Sioux*'s status improved. Train 11 was extended to Rapid City once again with a sleeper and streamlined coach from Chicago. The eastbound train from Rapid City was renumbered 2 and given an im-

On the re-equipped *Arrow* of 1929 a telephone was the prestige item of the limousine solarium-lounge. Of course, it could be used only before departure from Chicago or Omaha, but it represented modernity. Formal dress was not usually required of male passengers. — *Milwaukee Road.*

The Chicago-bound *Arrow* surmounts the 1 percent grade at Hill Siding south of Sioux Falls, South Dakota, in September 1950. Pacific 817 has a sheet steel pilot found on only a few F5s. Behind it are two 1947 headend cars, plus sleeping and diner-lounge cars out of sight around the curve. — *Marvin Nelson.*

Milwaukee-Chicago train 12 pauses at Sturtevant, Wisconsin, sometime in the early 1930s to receive passengers from the Southwestern local just visible to the left. Train 12 has an F3-class Pacific up front; in the middle of the train are a parlor car and a diner. — *A. Howard Christiansen.*

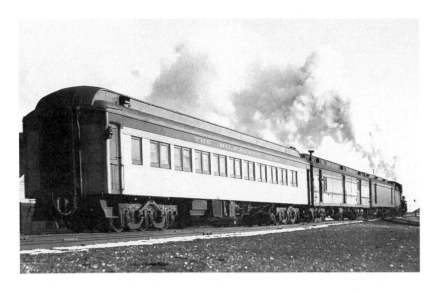

Berlin-Milwaukee afternoon local train 36 departs Ripon on March 29, 1947. Carrying the markers is a modernized air-conditioned coach; up front is Ten-Wheeler 1122. — *Clayton C. Tinkham.*

Typical of Milwaukee Road local trains at the time the *Hiawatha* was being designed and built, train 210 is shown at Franksville, Wisconsin, 19 miles south of Milwaukee, in February 1934, behind Atlantic type No. 3012. At Sturtevant the train will turn west onto the Southwestern toward Freeport, Illinois, and take the number 21. — *A. Howard Christiansen.*

proved schedule which connected with the *Midwest Hi*, creating a 23-hour journey from Rapid City to Chicago — 5 hours faster than the westbound *Sioux*. The eastbound *Sioux* became a Sioux Falls-Chicago train.

In August 1946 Pullman began operating the Minneapolis sleeping car, and in the spring of 1947 the use of streamlined coaches on 11 and 22, which had been sporadic during the war years, was again guaranteed.

For nearly all its career the *Sioux* was handled by Pacifics; west of Canton to Mitchell and Rapid City the trains were in the hands of class G Ten-Wheelers. Toward the end of steam, class F6 Hudsons were used occasionally on the *Sioux* in Iowa — bridge restrictions kept the 4-6-4s off the Madison-Marquette section. In 1947, the Iowa & Dakota division was dieselized west of Mitchell, S. Dak., with Alco RSC-2 road-switchers.

The *Sioux* improved further with restoration of the Chicago-Sioux Falls coach on train 11 in early 1948. In 1950 train 122, the Minneapolis section of the *Sioux*, was discontinued north of Austin, Minn., and in mid-January 1951, the *Marquettes*, trains 3 and 118 between Chicago and Mason City, Iowa, were discontinued. The road made several schedule changes, demonstrating a desire to mitigate the removal of trains. Train 11 was retimed to operate in the time slot vacated by train 3, about three hours later throughout

with an 8 a.m. arrival in Mason City, by then the most important city the train served. Train 22 ran one hour later, retaining convenient departure times from Sioux Falls and Mason City as well as from Madison, Wisconsin, where its new 7 a.m. departure replaced train 20, the *Varsity*. The *Marquette*, train 118, remained in service east of Madison, providing a late afternoon departure for Chicago, and it soon took on the *Varsity* name.

Since the westbound *Sioux* no longer had a dinner-hour departure from Chicago, its parlor-diner was removed. The eastbound *Sioux* continued to provide parlor and diner service using a car that moved to Madison via Milwaukee. The Chicago-Mason City sleeper and the Mason City-Sioux Falls diner-parlor were both discontinued in the summer of 1951.

September 30, 1951, saw the end of passenger train operation between Canton and Rapid City, S. Dak., and of the *Sioux* connections between Canton and Sioux Falls. The *Sioux* was now a fast train between Chicago and Madison, and a local between Madison and the Iowa-South Dakota border.

With the time change in the spring of 1952, the Chicago-Austin Pullman was permanently rerouted through La Crosse, Wis., and the Southern Minnesota line, although coach passengers could continue using the *Sioux* to and from Calmar, Iowa, where they changed to and from trains 103 and 122 —

In 1937 the railroad began air-conditioning conventional coaches, numbering them in the 4000s and referring to them as "modernized." Most interior appointments remained unchanged, but the cars received the same ceiling and recessed lighting as the 1937 streamlined coaches. The modernized cars were initially used to supplement streamlined coaches on non-*Hiawatha* intercity trains, and by 1940 they were for the most part assigned to locals and branchline trains. — *Both photos, Milwaukee Road.*

until the Calmar-Austin line became freight-only January 18, 1953.

In 1954 the Pullman Company took over operation of the *Sioux* sleeping car. The car ran only to Mason City, except on Sunday mornings, when it went on to Canton because there was no yard engine working at Mason City. Later the Mason City switcher became a five-day job, and stations west of there benefited from Pullman service Sundays and Mondays.

In October 1956, train 11's departure from Chicago was moved forward approximately two hours, making it more attractive as a Chicago-Madison conveyance, and a few months later, its parlor-diner was restored. The *Sioux* was discontinued west of Madison a few days after the beginning of 1960 and made its last Chicago-Madison runs April 30, 1971.

THE ARROW

Because the Chicago-Omaha line bypassed large cities, it was less passenger-oriented than the Twin Cities main line. However, the road fielded strong contenders in the limited era, and was ahead of its competition in introducing steam heat and electric lighting. By 1920 the principal train on the Illinois and Iowa divisions, 7 and 8, the *Omaha Limited* (later the *Omaha-Chicago Limited*), was duplicated except on the final 60 miles west of Manilla, Iowa, by trains 6 and 11, the *Sioux City Limited*.

August 1926 saw those four trains replaced by the *Arrow*, which retained the numbers 7 and 8 and was a double-destination train serving both Omaha and Sioux City. Sleepers ran Chicago-Des Moines (on connecting trains south of Madrid), Chicago-Omaha, Chicago-Sioux City, Milwaukee-Omaha (on the *Southwest Limited*, trains 25 and 26, east of Savanna), and Des Moines-Sioux Falls. The Des Moines-Sioux Falls car, which was carried on connecting trains north of Sioux City, was in the consist little more than a year. Club-observation cars ran between Chicago and Omaha, a dining car worked between Chicago and Savanna, and cafe-observations worked between Perry and Sioux City on Des Moines-Sioux City trains 107 and 108, which carried the *Arrow*'s Sioux City cars west of Perry. Chicago-Omaha run-

ning times were 13 hours 20 minutes; times to and from Sioux City were 45 minutes more.

In June 1929 the through trains between Des Moines and Sioux City made their last runs. They were replaced by Des Moines-Madrid and Manilla-Sioux City trains that made connections with Chicago-Omaha trains on the main line. At the same time, the sleeping cars from Des Moines to Chicago and from Omaha to Milwaukee were moved to train 20, the *Pacific Limited*, a through train from San Francisco via the Southern Pacific and Union Pacific railroads west of Omaha.

On July 26, 1929, the *Arrow* was given new roller-bearing-equipped cars. The feature car of the *Arrow* was a Chicago-Omaha limousine-lounge-observation car with valet service and a radio. Pullman took over operation of all the sleeping cars except the Des Moines-Sioux City car. The new sleeping cars had coil-spring mattresses throughout. Train 8's time had been shortened by an hour in June of that year, but the new roller-bearing-equipped cars brought no further reduction in the scheduled running time.

It's just after 5 p.m. on a late-1940s weekday in Milwaukee. Directly in front of us is F4 Pacific No. 885 on the "Cannonball" for Watertown and Madison. Two tracks over is Ten-Wheeler 1112 ready to leave with train 35 to Berlin. — *Truman Blasingame.*

Train 24, the *Traveler*, the premier morning train from Milwaukee to Chicago, charges through the reverse curve at Florida Street on Milwaukee's south side on a summer morning in 1950. Trains leaving Milwaukee southbound had to traverse several sharp curves and surmount a short but steep grade from the Menomonee River drawbridge to a stretch of track elevated above street level. Back around the curve are more coaches, a diner, and a parlor car. Class F6a engines such as 141 rarely strayed east of Minneapolis. Their straight running boards and pilot-deck air-pump shield distinguished them from the F6 class. The F6a engines had no air horn, just a genuine steam whistle. — *Jim Scribbins.*

Many would assert that the best passenger locomotives on the Milwaukee Road were the 70 class F3 Pacifics built by the Brooks works of American Locomotive Company in 1910. They yielded to nothing until the first Hudsons arrived 20 years later — and they did not fade away then. An F3 was designated to substitute if necessary for the initial pair of *Hiawatha* Atlantics, and two-thirds of the class remained active well into the 1950s. They regularly ran at 80 mph with Chicago-Milwaukee and Milwaukee-Madison trains, and when the occasion demanded they could and did make 90. F3 No. 163 is shown in charge of Milwaukee-Madison train 29 on a December 1947 afternoon. It has just crossed Harwood Avenue in Wauwatosa, leaving municipally imposed speed restrictions behind, and will have no difficulty at all cresting Brookfield Hill, the divide between the Lake Michigan and Mississippi River watersheds. The engineer will doubtless have to apply air for the speed restrictions for the Soo Line crossing at Duplainville and the curve at Hartland. It will cover the 33 miles from Milwaukee to Oconomowoc in 34 minutes. Oconomowoc to Watertown will be another 60-mph start-to-stop sprint, and it will average 60 over the branch to Sun Prairie. The only slow pace will be some street running in Madison at the end of the trip. — *Jim Scribbins.*

At Thanksgiving, the Omaha-to-Milwaukee and Des Moines-to-Chicago sleepers returned to train 8. The Sioux City-to-Des Moines sleeper schedule varied. For a while it was carried in the *Pacific Limited* between Manilla and Madrid. After that train's demise it was usually handled in local trains 104 and 4 before going down the branch to Des Moines, reaching there in the small hours of the morning.

When it was part of the eastbound *Arrow*, the car arrived around midnight. Passengers had the option of parlor car service, detraining on arrival and paying only for a seat; or higher-priced berth service with a full night's sleep before vacating the car at breakfast time.

In its final months the *Columbian*, the secondary Chicago-Tacoma train, was routed between Chicago and Aberdeen, S. Dak., via Manilla, Sioux City, and Mitchell. When it was discontinued in May 1931, a new connecting service with the *Olympian* was established — a Des Moines-Aberdeen sleeping car handled westbound on the *Arrow* between Madrid and Sioux City. Five months later, the southern terminal of the car was changed to Omaha. The

northbound car moved from Omaha to Manilla on local train 4, then from Manilla to Sioux City on the *Arrow*. The southbound car was carried on train 4 from Sioux City to Manilla (illustrating once again the Milwaukee Road's penchant for using the same train numbers over and over), then on the *Arrow* from Manilla to Omaha.

Two years later the run became a tourist sleeper line, and briefly in 1937 the sleeper was designated as a buffet-tourist car. Whether a long-dormant range was activated or a new one was installed so the porter could also act as chef is unknown. (At one time tourist sleepers had a small kitchen so passengers could cook their own meals.)

Even this obscure car line was altered by inauguration of the *Midwest Hiawatha* in December 1940. A side effect of the new speedliner was discontinuance of Omaha-Chicago local 104 and its connection from Sioux City. The result was another case of a freight train becoming a mixed. Time freight 64 carried the sleeper and a coach from Sioux City to Manilla in order to reach the westbound *Arrow* for Omaha. Curiously, the equipment listing did not

On a summer day in 1949 Train 29 is about to slam across the Soo Line diamond at Duplainville, 17 miles west of Milwaukee, with *Hiawatha* Atlantic No. 4 doing the honors. — *Jim Scribbins*.

show a coach from Sioux City to Manilla, but the schedule column noted that "coach passengers will be carried on No. 64 from Sioux City to Manilla." Later the railroad relented and added a coach to the equipment listing. An even stranger circumstance occurred between 1946 and 1948: Chicago & North Western 2-201, the *Nightingale*, its principal overnight Twin Cities-Omaha train, carried Milwaukee's Aberdeen-Omaha tourist car from Sioux City to Omaha during its final two years. The move was not mentioned in C&NW public timetables.

In 1930 the *Arrow* received a Chicago telephone in its lounge car prior to departure. This prestigious item had its number listed in the city phone book. From March 29, 1931, the *Arrow* — with one brief westbound exception — was permanently consolidated with the *Southwest Limited* between Chicago and Savanna.

The *Arrow* was extended to Sioux Falls from Sioux City in early summer 1934. The running time of train 7 was reduced significantly, and both the Omaha and Sioux Falls lounge cars, as well as the Chicago-Savanna dining

car, were air-conditioned. In October, streamlined coaches were assigned to both the Omaha and Sioux Falls runs.

Early in 1935, the Chicago-Omaha limousine-lounge-observations were replaced by 3-double-bedroom, 1-compartment, lounge cars, and by summer the *Arrow* was fully air-conditioned. In 1937, the *Arrow*'s train numbers were changed to 107-108 Chicago-Omaha and 117-118 Manilla-Sioux Falls. In the spring of 1938 the sleeper-lounge was switched to the Chicago-Sioux Falls run, and for less than three months a Des Moines-Omaha Pullman was operated.

Even though F6 Hudsons had been used since the early 1930s, the *Arrow*'s schedules never became as fast as those of the *Pioneer Limited*, and remained 12 to 13 hours for the life of the train. Local trains 103 and 104 between Chicago and Omaha stopped running with the coming of the *Midwest Hiawatha*, and 107 and 108 had to absorb their express and mail cars and — for a few months — their station stops as well. By 1946, class S3 4-8-4s had been assigned to the *Arrow* and remained on the train well into 1949. The Manilla-Sioux Falls section was in the hands of 800 series 4-6-2s originally built for Lines West.

In mid-1946 the Milwaukee-Omaha sleeper operation was transferred to the railroad from Pullman. Fall 1948 saw the end of dining car service between Omaha and Manilla. In early 1949 Des Moines-Sioux City, Chicago-Des Moines, and Milwaukee-Omaha sleeping cars were all discontinued.

By 1953 Sioux City and Sioux Falls were more important to the *Arrow* than Omaha and Council Bluffs. Streamlined sleeping cars came to the Sioux Falls portion of the *Arrow* in September 1953, at first 10-roomette, 6-bedroom cars, then through all of 1954 14-roomette, 2-drawing-room cars. In January 1955, duplex-roomette cars from the *Pioneer Limited* were assigned to the Chicago-Sioux Falls run and the Chicago-Omaha sleeper was discontinued.

On "Union Pacific day," October 30, 1955, the Chicago-Omaha sleeper was reinstated, and the train was renumbered 109 and 110. Three months later it was again renumbered to 19 and 20. The Omaha sleeper was dropped again in September 1958. Between October 1956 and September 1959 the *Arrow* carried a Chicago-Los Angeles coach that operated west of Omaha in Union Pacific secondary trains.

The Manilla-Sioux Falls portion of the train was discontinued September 17, 1965, as was the lunch-lounge car running between Chicago and Savanna. The *Arrow* became a coach-only Chicago-Omaha train; it made its last runs October 5, 1967.

THE FAST MAIL AND EXPRESS

The Milwaukee Road operated one of the most famous mail and express trains in the United States, train 57. The train was regularly listed in the road's passenger timetables with the note, "Does not carry passengers or baggage." (For a while, however, it carried as far as La Crosse a sleeper and a coach destined to Austin, Minn.) Curiously, its opposite number, train 56, did carry passengers. So important were the pair that when CMStP&P first employed mainline diesels they and one *Hiawatha* each way were the first to be entrusted to the new power. Engine 15, the road's only EMD E6, had the tough assignment of taking 57 to Minneapolis each night, then returning to Chicago with train 6, the *Morning Hiawatha* — an extremely heavy, fast mail train in one direction and the second-fastest train in North America in the other. Alco DL-109 No. 14 faced a task that was only slightly less arduous:

Afternoon *Hiawatha* 101 to the Twin Cities and return on *Fast Mail* 56.

In the 1940s and 1950s train 57 carried three working Railway Post Office cars; only the Boston-Washington run exceeded that number. As recently as the 1960s, Donald M. Steffee, international rail operations analyst, considered train 57 to be one of the ten most demanding schedules on this planet!

It was difficult to start a heavy westbound train from Milwaukee's Everett Street station. Fifty-seven's engine would be in the intersection of Fifth and Clybourn streets, with its first few cars on the curve at the west end of the station. From about the tenth car back, everything was on the sharp curve at the east end of the station through the intersection of Second and Clybourn, and a long 57 could have its markers back across Plankinton Avenue almost to the Menomonee River drawbridge on yet another curve. To the west were a curve as the train emerged from beneath the Sixth Street viaduct, and a final bend at about Eighth Street.

It diminishes neither man nor machine — even E6 No. 15 — to acknowledge that a depot switcher was often called to assist. The east end depot engine, 600 h.p. EMD SW1 No. 1630, would attach the Wisconsin Valley cars behind 57's unique crew rider car and break its air-hose connection but remain coupled to the train. When the two long blasts of engine 15's air horn announced the highball, engineer Kelley on the SW1 would open his throttle and off they would go in unison, No. 1630 in the top notch, spinning its wheels and dumping sand in quantity. By the time the SW1 entered the train shed, the E6 on the head end would have matters well in hand, and a switchman on the front of the SW1 would lift the pin. About Third Street, the *Fast Mail and Express* would pull ahead, Kelley would close his throttle and apply the engine brake. Fifty-seven was on the road!

CHICAGO-MILWAUKEE-MADISON TRAINS

The network of fast trains the Milwaukee Road operated in later years in the Chicago-Milwaukee-Madison triangle evolved slowly.

In the 1890s significant and effective intercity service began between Chicago and Milwaukee with six trains in each direction. Most trains needed two and one-quarter hours, but train 23, the afternoon train from Chicago to Milwaukee, made the run in less than two hours.

The Chicago-Milwaukee service gradually increased in frequency, but it was never faster than 105 minutes until the *Hiawatha* era. In fact, after having achieved an almost uniform two-hour running time by 1910, several trains had their times lengthened by 15 minutes when class F3 Pacifics succeeded Atlantics as the principal passenger locomotive — apparently the Pacifics had difficulty with long trains of steel cars.

It's Christmastime 1948. Train 33, the *On Wisconsin* from Milwaukee, is on the last lap of its trip, from Franklin Street station near the state capitol to the principal Madison station on West Washington Avenue, where the RPO-express car behind the tender will be switched to Madison Division train 33 to continue west to Marquette, Iowa. In the conventional parlor-diner the waiter and the chef are washing up the breakfast dishes. — *William D. Middleton.*

Madison, Wisconsin, is known to students of railroad engineering for the intersection of the Milwaukee Road and the Chicago & North Western in Lake Monona. Train 118, the *Varsity*, has just begun its trip to Chicago as it clatters over the diamond at Monona Tower. In a few minutes the *Dakota 400* will come directly toward the photographer, also Chicago-bound, passing what its railway designates as Tower MX.
— *William D. Middleton.*

Wilson Street on Madison's east side is one of the few places the Milwaukee Road engages in street running. This is Saturday-only train 47 from Milwaukee in late March 1952. — *Edward P. Wilkomen.*

On a spring day in 1949 Alco DL-109 No. 14A scoots through the western fringes of Wauwatosa, Wisconsin, with Madison-Milwaukee-Chicago train 46, on time and doing a mile a minute. The raised "Milwaukee Road" lettering beneath the silver wings has been simply painted over and the grillwork over the radiator shutters is missing — the road's second passenger diesel is no longer a star of the fleet. — *Jim Scribbins.*

In 1914, the CM&StP had on its drawing boards at West Milwaukee Shops a 4-6-2 which would have been 25 percent more powerful than an F3. That locomotive was never built, but the design evolved into the first-planned North American 4-6-4. The path from mechanical department to erecting shop was a long one, particularly for a railway as financially unstable as the Milwaukee, and New York Central had its first Hudson, No. 5200, on the rails three years ahead of CMStP&P's class F6 4-6-4.

Direct Chicago-Madison service began in 1900, when the road opened a cutoff from Libertyville, Ill., to Janesville, Wis., creating a Chicago-Madison route 28 miles shorter than the route through Milwaukee and Watertown. Three trains in each direction were established with parlor and buffet service, but only one of those trains could be described as anything other than a local. In 1927, the morning train to Madison and the afternoon return to Chicago were named the *Varsity*, and the next year a similarly timed pair of Milwaukee-Madison trains received the title *On Wisconsin*. The *On Wisconsin* and an unnamed pair of trains on the same route were quickened to two hours by

eliminating all intermediate stops except Oconomowoc and Watertown.

Chicago-Milwaukee service reached its zenith in January 1942 with 14 trains each way every day. Seven in each direction were scheduled over the 85 miles in 75 minutes, and only three northbound and five southbound trains required more than 85 minutes to scoot across the C&M Subdivision. All but four trips were powered by steam locomotives.

Trains 5 and 6 ran between Chicago and the Twin Cities, carrying a parlor car and requiring about 15 hours for their journey. West of Milwaukee they halted at nearly every station. Running times of these trains remained about the same until the advent of the 6400 series F6 Hudsons in 1930, although by then they had been titled the *Day Express* for quite a few years and carried dining and observation cars.

Trains serving Madison, the capital of Wisconsin, became streamliners as cars from prewar *Hiawatha*s came to secondary passenger trains on the entire system — though they acquired *Grove*-series parlor-diners fresh out of Milwaukee Shops. Some Milwaukee-Madison trains approached *Hiawatha* stan-

69

dards by wheeling 82 miles in 85 minutes despite 2 intermediate stops, 26 miles of branch line, and street running on Madison's east side. Chicago-Madison times were about the same on the direct route through Janesville and on the long way around through Milwaukee because of the higher speeds possible on the main line.

When the westbound *Sioux*'s schedule was adjusted to compensate for the end of the *Marquette*, train 7-111 from Chicago through Milwaukee to Madison received a former *Hi* tap car and a parlor car to encourage the after-business-hours trade. Train 118, the late-afternoon train from Madison to Chicago via Janesville, carried a tap car and a parlor-diner. In April 1951, it was renamed the *Varsity* and received a Beaver Tail and a tap-diner from the 1935 *Hi*. The 1938 tap car which had been running on 118 now returned to Chicago on midday 106 to Milwaukee and on train 46 from there to Chicago. These consists represented the pinnacle of diesel-era Madison passenger train service.

Fall 1951 brought substitution of a *Grove*-series parlor-diner for the Beaver Tail and tap-diner on 117 and 118; and 106 and 7-111 said good-bye to their tap car, though the latter's parlor remained, as did its Chicago-Milwaukee diner. Two years later, Milwaukee-Madison trains 29 and 112 were discontinued, and trains 33 and 14, the *On Wisconsin*, made their final trips early in March 1955 (they had lost their *Camp*-series heavyweight diner-parlor-solarium in September 1949). That left only trains 23, 106, and 111 on the Milwaukee-Madison run.

For many years, the timetable gave the appearance of one more train to Madison than returned. Train 23 served not only as a Chicago-Madison train, but also as a Milwaukee-Watertown commuter run. The locomotive, two forward cars, and the crew remained at Watertown overnight to return to Milwaukee the next morning as local train 12. At Watertown, an engine, branch line combine, and crew that had come east from Madison as local freight 432 took 23's Madison cars back to the state capital.

Occasionally eastbound freight work was heavy on the branch and train 432 would reach Watertown with barely enough time to turn. In such instances, the crew went back to Madison in their freight clothes, not passenger uniforms. This interesting quirk ceased with the termination of all Milwaukee-Madison passenger trains February 18, 1957. On that date, the *Grove* car which had run to Madison on 23 was transferred to the westbound *Sioux*.

The two Chicago-Janesville-Madison trains operated with little change until spring 1964 when 117 and 118, the *Varsity*, had its parlor-diner replaced

with a tap-grill car, then five months later with a Super Dome. Another surplus Super Dome made morning and afternoon round trips between Chicago and Milwaukee on trains 27, 12, 23, and 58. These assignments lasted only until spring 1965, when the domes on both routes and the *Grove* car on the *Sioux* were discontinued.

In the fall of 1968, because of steadily declining use, the *Varsity* became a Friday-Saturday-Sunday university-oriented operation. The *Sioux* continued to operate daily, to Chicago in the morning and back to Madison in the evening. The Chicago-Janesville-Madison trains were not among the trains Amtrak included in its system on May 1, 1971.

The last remnant of Milwaukee-Madison service was the Milwaukee-Watertown commuter train, Nos. 12 and 23, known locally as the "Cannonball," at first perhaps as a term of derision but later with fondness. It survived more than a year into the Amtrak era; it was discontinued July 31, 1972.

Attrition of Chicago-Milwaukee service was largely a matter of the discontinuance of through trains such as the *Chippewa-Hiawatha*, the *Afternoon Hiawatha*, and the *Pioneer Limited*. When Amtrak took over operation of the nation's passenger trains on May 1, 1971, the road was still operating three Chicago-Milwaukee round trips, two daily and the third daily except Sunday. Chicago-Milwaukee passengers could also take advantage of the *Morning Hiawatha* and the eastbound *Fast Mail*.

EMPLOYEE TRAINS

The last employee trains on CMStP&P operated between the coach yard and roundhouse at Western Avenue, Chicago, and the classification yard and engine terminal at Bensenville. They were shown in the employees' timetable as Second Class, unusual for passenger runs, and were permitted to leave their initial stations without a dispatcher's clearance. As late as 1946, six round trips were operated every day, all but one between 10 p.m. and 7 a.m. During daytime hours, many commuter trains stopped for employees at the Bensenville roundhouse and yard office, and the Western Avenue coach yard was easily reached from the commuter station there. A few trains stopped as well at the roundhouse at the north end of the Western Avenue complex. By 1959 the coach runs, as the timetable designated them, had dwindled to two round trips daily, before the start of the day and afternoon shifts. About 1960 a company bus was substituted for the trains; later, railroaders had to rely on commuter trains or their own automobiles.

A September 1950 afternoon finds the sole daytime employee train approaching Bensenville, Illinois, station behind a seven-year-old Alco RS-1. The turn-of-the-century wood coaches have been painted boxcar red and carry reporting marks and numbers below the windows, indicating they are non-revenue equipment. Carrying the markers of this second-class passenger train is a cupola caboose. — *Jim Scribbins*.

MOTOR CARS

Around the turn of the century, the electric interurban railway, a long-distance adaptation of the streetcar, achieved a measure of success as a passenger-carrying competitor to railroads. The Milwaukee Electric Railway & Light Company, for example, effectively replaced the Milwaukee Road's local trains between Milwaukee and Waukesha and siphoned off a significant amount of Oconomowoc and Watertown riders as well. Because of this competition, the Milwaukee Road had little difficulty discontinuing its Milwaukee-Waukesha local passenger trains.

Generally, though, railroads needed a more efficient form of operation for rural local trains which were, even then, money losers but which could not be discontinued due to the resistance of regulatory commissions.

During the 1890s the gasoline engine began to be contemplated as a prime mover for self-propelled railway cars. Development of the automobile led to substantial improvement of this energy source and during the first years of the new century the petroleum-powered railcar became practical.

The most dependable motor cars were those built by General Electric. They had a gasoline engine driving a generator which sent electricity to turn the traction motors on the car's front truck. The cars generally became known as "gas-electrics," and the manner in which they linked gasoline engine with flanged wheel was the same as that later used in diesel-electric locomotives.

Self-propulsion meant railroads no longer would be obliged to place even a small, elderly steam locomotive with an engineer and fireman on a branchline train of one head-end car and a largely unoccupied coach. A single self-propelled car could carry mail, express, and passengers. Moreover, it could be operated with only an engineer, a conductor, and, in some instances, a brakeman-baggageman. When the run was finished, the car's engine could simply be shut down. Because the gasoline engine was more efficient than the steam locomotive, and the weight of the motor car vastly less than that of its predecessor, cost reductions beyond wage savings could be effected. It was clear that motor cars, as they were generally designated within railroading, would be a welcome aid in holding branchline passenger train losses to acceptable levels.

Five motor cars were purchased in 1912 and 1913 for the Milwaukee Road proper and two for the Chicago, Milwaukee & Puget Sound. Their gasoline engines and electrical components were from General Electric. GE's electrical equipment had been proven in street railway and interurban operation, and the gas engines were relatively satisfactory. The bodies were built by Wason Manufacturing Company, a Springfield, Massachusetts, subsidiary of Philadelphia's well-known Brill streetcar concern, and were of two body types: express-coach and RPO-express-coach.

In 1914 one car made seven round trips daily between Racine and Sturtevant (then known as Corliss), Wisconsin, 7½ miles, to connect with C&M and Southwestern trains. Single cars operated daily between Wabasha and Faribault, Minnesota, 188 miles round trip; Hastings-Cologne, Minn., 112 miles; Canton-Egan, South Dakota, 110 miles; and Seattle-Enumclaw,

One of Milwaukee Road's General Electric motor cars makes a station stop at Monticello, Iowa. The engineer sat not directly behind the windshield but beside the open window above the rear axle of the front truck. For a while in the 1920s this pleasant community was served by motor cars from Davenport, Cedar Rapids, and Calmar. — *Milwaukee Road.*

The electrification was scarcely five years old when the road converted three General Electric motor cars to trolley maintenance cars, replacing caboose-like cars pulled by steam engines. In turn, the GE cars were replaced by an ex-Northwestern Pacific motor car built in 1930, and ultimately by hi-rail trucks. — *Milwaukee Road.*

Locomotor 5942 is shown at Cedar Rapids, Iowa, shortly after it was acquired in 1931. The car has an express room and an RPO apartment. Behind the car are two wood coaches and a company-owned sleeping car. — *Milwaukee Road.*

Milwaukee-Berlin (Wisconsin) trains 31 and 36 were handled by streamlined motor car 5900 from May 1948 until they were replaced by trains 30 and 35 in June 1950. Train 31 is shown approaching Center Street in Milwaukee on a grade which saw occasional freight helpers. On the rear of the train is the combine for the mixed train between Horicon and Portage. — *Jim Scribbins.*

Washington, 123 miles. Two cars were needed on the Everett, Wash., branch. One camped for the night in North Bend and started its day by going down to Cedar Falls to meet the Enumclaw train, then traveled over the entire branch to Everett, then returned to Cedar Falls and North Bend for a total of 126 miles. The other car, based at Everett, made five round trips to Monroe, 14 miles each way, carrying employees of the many Everett sawmills to and from their suburban homes.

Though General Electric was a leader in motor cars, the technology was still new and cars 5900-5906 were at times cantankerous — as all their breed seemed. Ultimately their use declined. By 1926, three of the cars had been converted to trolley line maintenance cars, but the road's Mechanical Department credited the remaining four with giving a good account of themselves on Lines East.

CM&StP introduced the first North American diesel-powered motor car on October 12, 1927, when a Foos six-cylinder L-type 200 h.p. engine was installed in car 5906. The diesel engine offered better fuel economy and reduced the risk of engine room fires. The car was operated as train 27, which had an early morning departure from Calmar, Iowa, ran south to Monticello, and after a long layover returned by mid-evening to Calmar.

Interest in motor cars continued, principally because of their economy. In 1928 the road acquired 15 cars from the Electro-Motive Corporation. Cars 5925-5934 were the first EMC cars to have bodies built by Standard Steel Car Company; cars 5935-5939 were built by Pullman. Most had an express-coach configuration, but in 1929 cars 5925-5934 were changed to express-Railway Post Office. Passengers were accommodated in trailing elderly 3800-series coaches. Cars 5935 and 5936 were converted to RPO-coach configuration, while 5937 and 5939 retained their original form. Number 5938 had been constructed as a triple-purpose vehicle.

Milwaukee Road's ownership of motor cars peaked at 21 in 1931, and the motor car schedules of that time required 18 cars. By then the Hastings-Cologne and Wabasha-Faribault runs had been replaced by mixed trains, and the Racine-Corliss shuttle was by then a bus. All but one of the services could be covered by a single car making a round trip each day. In retrospect it might have been better, considering the uneven temperament of the beasts, to assign two cars to the longer runs to ease the rigors of daily work. Some runs operated daily, but most were scheduled Monday through Saturday.

Chicago, Terre Haute & Southeastern ran a Terre Haute-Bedford, Indiana, job. Milwaukee was served by cars from Freeport, Illinois, and Janesville, Wis., while another duo made trips between Rockford, Ill., and Portage, Wis., with additional turnarounds at each end: Portage-Madison and Rockford-Janesville.

Savanna, Ill., fielded cars to La Crosse, Wis., via Dubuque, Iowa, and to Davenport, Iowa, by way of the east side of the Mississippi River. The latter car began its southbound run by going east to Lanark, then down the Ashdale cutoff. In Iowa motor cars operated between Cedar Rapids and Ottumwa, Cedar Rapids and Calmar, and Des Moines and Spirit Lake — two trips in each direction on the last named.

The southern Minnesota junction of Wells sent motor trains north to St. Paul and west to Jackson. Sioux City and Sioux Falls were linked by trains 307 and 308, and the Platte line west from Yankton, S. Dak., offered "doodlebug" service. The only motor car service in the far west was over the former Idaho & Washington Northern between Spokane and Metaline Falls.

Early on an overcast Saturday morning, July 27, 1957, motor car 5900 brings train 30, consisting of a single 1935 lightweight coach, past a pond into Ripon, Wisconsin. — *Clayton C. Tinkham.*

On Independence Day 1951 motor car 5931, uniquely painted with a broad maroon window band, and a 1937 combine await a 6:20 p.m. departure from Spirit Lake, Iowa, for the 178-mile run to Des Moines. On the way train 36 will connect with train 22, the *Sioux*, at Spencer, and train 108, the *Arrow*, at Herndon. The 40-seat combine will be more than adequate for the passenger load, and the train will run for the last time on April 12, 1952. — *William W. Kratville.*

Two cars, 5941 and 5942, covered the only run which required two days for a round trip — trains 3 and 8 between Davenport and Kansas City. These cars were the highly unusual Locomotors, produced by the joint efforts of International Harvester, a builder of agricultural implements; the Ryan Car Company, a Chicago builder of freight cars; and Pullman, which built the bodies. Two eight-cylinder uniflow steam engines developing a total of 450 h.p. were mounted beneath the floor to power the front and rear trucks. In the customary gasoline engine location inside the operator's cab was an oil-fired boiler producing steam at between 600 and 650 pounds per square inch, considerably higher than that produced by any locomotive on the road. Exhaust steam was condensed for reuse in a large condensing unit occupying about forty percent of the roof space of the Locomotor. It was felt the steam cars could be operated at higher speeds than the gas-electrics. Further, the en-

gineer would be more at home with controls similar to those of a steam locomotive and he would be working in a quieter location than the cab of an internal-combustion-powered car.

Car 5941 was first tried in 1929 between Milwaukee and Mineral Point, Wis., running opposite a conventional steam train on a round trip requiring two days. A local resident remembered it as pulling one coach and being extremely quiet. He also recalled how No. 5941 was frequently towed behind a Ten-Wheeler. The road acquired car 5942 in 1931 after it had served as a demonstrator for Ryan-Harvester. On April 7 of that year, it made a Chicago-Elgin round trip in a bit less than two hours, including several intermediate stops, achieving a top speed of 55 mph. Number 5942's first regular service was on the Cedar Rapids-Ottumwa line, but by late May it had been placed opposite its twin in Davenport-Kansas City service. While this run was appar-

Motor car 5930 eases away from Brookfield, Wisconsin, in June 1949, having just entered the La Crosse Division main line from the original Milwaukee & Mississippi line. It left Janesville at 9:05 a.m., after receiving passengers from the Madison-Chicago *Varsity*, and will be in Milwaukee in another 26 minutes. Passengers are treated to the luxury of a 1942 *Hiawatha* coach.
— *Jim Scribbins.*

ently permanent for the duo, one of the Locomotors briefly ran out of Milwaukee during March 1937.

The unique cars proved to be less reliable than the gas-electrics. Their chief difficulty was that materials available at the time could not withstand the intense heat needed to produce flash steam at 600 pounds per square inch pressure. The boilers sprang leaks, and neither builder nor road was able to develop a burner capable of producing the required high-pressure steam. After mounting costs and undependable operation, ultimately the pair was retired.

Perhaps to fill the void created by the retirement of the Locomotors, CMStP&P purchased two Southern Pacific motor cars in 1941: 5940 and second 5941. The latter was made into a line car for use in the electric zones and served in that role until 1965, outlasting all the Milwaukee Road's other motor cars. Operation of gas-electrics in revenue passenger service on the Milwaukee Road ceased with the final trips of trains 23 and 24 between Cedar Rapids and Calmar, Iowa, on August 12, 1954.

Even in 1947, when the postwar surge in automobile ownership had not yet taken its big bite from rail passenger miles, passenger train losses ate up about one-third of net operating income produced by freight service. Much of that loss was incurred by branchline trains. Since state regulatory commissions were sensitive to local opinion and rail labor attitudes, it was exceedingly difficult at the time to discontinue money-losing rural trains. The Milwaukee Road made one last attempt to use motor cars.

In the spring of 1948, Milwaukee Shops produced streamlined cars 5900 and 5901. Sometimes called "bulldogs" due to their flat noses, the pair were painted orange and trimmed with maroon and gray plus a vertical chrome strip surrounding their headlights. Each car's front end, including cab, was essentially that of a freight diesel. Behind was a motor room containing an Electro-Motive model 12-567-A 1,000 h.p. diesel engine. The rest of the car was an express compartment. EMD also provided the generator and traction motors, enabling all propulsion equipment to be interchangeable with contemporary EMD passenger locomotives and reducing the road's parts inventory. Numbers 5900 and 5901 were carried on two six-wheel trucks, the front truck powered with two traction motors. The pair cost approximately $150,000 each, but anticipated savings compared with steam trains were estimated to be $50,000 annually per motor car. When the cars rolled off the Milwaukee Shops transfer table it was remarked that RPO rooms could be partitioned off from the express space. Actually, for whatever reason, the rear portions of the cars never seem to have been used for express and were just so much empty space and added weight during their twelve-year existence.

On Monday, May 3, 1948, No. 5900 was tested between Milwaukee and Madison in nonrevenue service. Later that month it was assigned to trains 31

and 36 between Milwaukee and Berlin, Wis., with a regular consist of a standard heavyweight RPO-express and a heavyweight coach. Between Milwaukee and Horicon, 54 miles, the combine for Horicon-Portage mixed trains 531 and 536 tagged along, so between those points the train approximated the weight of the four streamlined cars the new motor was designed to pull. The closely spaced local stops and the 50 mph maximum speed imposed by the timetable kept the flashy unit well below its 75 mph maximum.

Number 5900 spent virtually its entire life on the original Northern division (by then the Third District of the Milwaukee Division) with occasional brief stints on the "Cannonball" between Milwaukee and Watertown, Wis. It was eventually assigned to trains 30 and 35 between Milwaukee and Berlin and remained on that run until the trains were discontinued in 1958.

By mid-June, 5901 was out of the shops, and for a while it pulled Milwaukee-Berlin trains, 30 and 35. They were slightly faster than 31 and 36 and carried a streamlined coach (usually one of the 4400-series cars of 1934) and a conventional RPO-express car. Car 5901 was soon transferred to trains 117 and 118 between Harlowton and Great Falls, Montana, remaining on that job until the trains were discontinued in August 1955.

When northern Montana passenger service ceased, 5901 returned to the Midwest for duty on trains 157 and 158 between La Crosse, Wis., and Austin, Minn., until that last southern Minnesota varnish took down its markers forever in March 1960. Number 5901 was brought to Milwaukee to head commuter trains 12 and 23 but the "Cannonball" schedule was too demanding — as it had been for 5900 — and the homebuilts were permanently sidelined for the greater accelerative capabilities of FP7s.

The goal of using streamlined motor cars to reduce costs was a valid one, but the Milwaukee had unknowingly already found a more flexible tool for eradicating branchline passenger losses when it adopted American Locomotive Company's RSC-2 road-switchers elsewhere on the system in 1947, a year before 5900 and 5901 entered the scene.

This view of the cab of the motor car powering train 23 on its last trip from Calmar to Cedar Rapids, Iowa, on August 12, 1954, shows that the engineer of a gas-electric was on intimate terms with the machine he controlled. There were many cooler, quieter places in Iowa that August afternoon. — *Don Hofsommer.*

The F7s and F9s were Milwaukee Road's freight workhorses for more than a decade. A quartet of Fs in A-B-B-A formation and wearing the black-edged maroon band powers a freight westbound through Pewaukee, Wisconsin, in May 1965. — *Robert W. Ferge.*

THE COLORFUL
MILWAUKEE ROAD

Train 106 to Milwaukee awaits its last departure from Madison, Wisconsin, behind E7 19A on February 17, 1957. — *Stanley H. Mailer.*

Quill motor E-13 leads the *Olympian* through the Bitterroots in the early 1940s. — *Milwaukee Road.*

The Milwaukee Road displayed bipolar No. E-3 at the 1948 Chicago Railroad Fair. On its way east from its usual assignment between Tacoma, Seattle, and Othello, it was shown off in Milwaukee. — *Lew Martin*.

The contours of Skytop parlor car *Coon Rapids* are displayed at their best in this overhead view of the 1948 version of the *Afternoon Hiawatha*, taken just north of Glenview, Illinois. — *Milwaukee Road.*

Veteran F3-class Pacific 171 poses at Monona Tower in Madison, Wisconsin, on May 23, 1954, with an excursion train sponsored by the Milwaukee Chapter of the National Railway Historical Society to commemorate the centennial of Milwaukee-Madison rail service. — *Russ Porter.*

Many of Milwaukee's first-generation diesel models are represented in this June 1965 scene at the Milwaukee engine terminal: E7, F7, FP7, GP9, H12-44, H16-44, SW1, and SW1200. — *Robert W. Ferge.*

Class S2 4-8-4 No. 207, one of 20 such machines built in 1937, crests the summit of the grade south out of Milwaukee at Lake Tower with a freight train for Chicago about 1950. — *Russ Porter.*

New F7s 75 and 76 stand side by side at Bensenville, Illinois in 1950. Behind them rises the skeleton of a new diesel house. — *Russ Porter.*

Only a handful of railroads purchased Fairbanks-Morse C-Liners. The first of Milwaukee's six 3-unit sets is shown on a freight train near 7 Mile Road in Caledonia, Wisconsin, in August 1963. — *Russ Porter.*

CITY TICKET OFFICES

As cities increased in size and population density during the 1880s and 1890s, railroads realized that in addition to their stations, they needed more convenient establishments to sell tickets to long-distance riders. Frequently, major stations were located away from a city's business, financial, and hotel districts. Chicago Union Station was some distance from the "Loop"; in Milwaukee, the business district moved away from the locations of the first three stations. Similar circumstances were to be found in other cities on the Milwaukee Road.

This meant the office of the businessman, the chief user of the trains and the sleeping car accommodations, was usually not near the passenger station, and planning and ticketing a trip required a lengthy absence by a secretary, office manager, or even the executive himself.

Downtown or city ticket offices, situated as close as possible to their clients, were introduced to reduce the time needed to arrange a trip. The city offices were most often in a principal office building, and sometimes in first-class hotels. Since such offices were not racing the clock by selling tickets for departing trains, the atmosphere was more leisurely than at a station. Clerks could take the time to thoroughly plan an itinerary and explain the intricacies of coupon tickets. The offices were spacious, with large open counters — considerably more appealing than the barred ticket windows found in most stations. A variety of seating was available, eliminating the lines and crowding often experienced at station ticket offices. City offices also provided a more pleasant setting than the station for women who were mapping out the details of their trips.

Railroads often maintained city offices in important municipalities not on their lines. The Milwaukee Road, for example, had off-line offices in Vancouver, British Columbia, and Cincinnati, Ohio.

An important aspect of the city ticket office was that all its salesmanship could be oriented toward the road's own trains. Imagine the neutrality and diplomacy required of a ticket clerk in St. Paul Union Depot (an employee of the station company rather than a railroad employee) selling tickets for five railroads to Chicago and three to Puget Sound, with limiteds departing within minutes of one another. At the Milwaukee Road's city office, clerks could recommend the *Pioneer Limited*, the *Olympian*, and — in more modern times — the *Hiawatha* without restraint.

A city ticket agent was charged with direct supervision of the staff, running a smoothly functioning office, and interpretation of the more intricate details of tariffs when information and ticket clerks met with a problem. He gained his expertise by coming up through the ranks: information-reservation clerk, ticket clerk, and possibly a stint as sales representative.

City ticket offices attracted clerks with the greatest length of service, since duty in a city office meant only normal daytime business hours with Sundays off — station ticket office work involved all three shifts and weekends. Information and reservation clerks were often one and the same, working at a

For many years the Milwaukee city ticket office was on the southeast corner of Wisconsin Avenue and East Water Street in the Iron Block Building, now a registered historic landmark. The Chicago, Milwaukee & Puget Sound lettering on the windows indicates this photo was taken in 1911 or 1912. The Union Pacific and a steamship company also had space in the office. — *Milwaukee Road*.

Inside the Milwaukee city ticket office, clients encountered steam heat, electric lights, tile floor, highly polished counters, and couches and chairs to make waiting easier. Framed views of scenery along the Milwaukee Road's lines hung on the walls. — *Milwaukee Road*.

portion of the counter reserved for inquiries. They would explain the various styles of sleeping accommodations, differentiate between coach and parlor seating, plan itineraries, and then, when the traveler was certain of his or her plans, request reservations. Usually ticket clerks helped patrons plan trips, but a major city office had one or more information clerks to ensure that some of the ticket clerks were always available to issue tickets to patrons with confirmed reservations.

Since much business and pleasure travel involved more than one railroad, many transactions were necessitated between connecting lines to complete the ticketing for an extended trip. When a ticket or information clerk completed an itinerary for a passenger, a written request for reservations was turned over to the reservation clerk, who would assign accommodations on the Milwaukee's own trains, or contact the foreign lines. In the Twin Cities or Milwaukee, for example, filling of most reservations was done by telephone.

CMStP&P personnel would phone the reservation offices of connecting lines to obtain a roomette on the *Broadway* or the *Century*, a bedroom on the *Dixieland*, a parlor car seat on the *Alton Limited*, or whatever. A steady procession of telegrams and teletype messages would move to and from the office requesting space on trains returning from distant points — along both coasts for example. When all of the answers were received, the descriptions of the accommodations — the "space," to use the railroad term — were entered on a single form (filed in accordance with the departure date from the originating station) and the tickets were issued.

One or more sales representatives, generally designated as passenger agents, worked out of the city ticket office. A city agent made sales calls within the metropolitan area, while a traveling man roamed a wider geographic area. These representatives not only sought travelers from business firms but actively worked with fraternal groups, schools, professional sports clubs, and

other organizations which could be expected to fill special cars or special trains. When vaudeville was alive, there were sales representatives who worked full time with the entertainment world. Sales staff, like supervisors, were usually promoted from the ranks of ticket and information clerks.

Several city offices also housed people holding titles such as general agent–passenger department or assistant general passenger agent, and those offices were the regional headquarters for passenger sales and service. The Milwaukee office, for example, had jurisdiction over most of Wisconsin; the Minneapolis office over Minnesota, the extreme western and northwestern part of Wisconsin, and the Dakotas. General agents coordinated the city and station offices and kept an overview of smaller towns. In the railroad hierarchy, the assistant general passenger agent was one step below the general passenger agent (in later years passenger traffic manager), the road's top passenger officer.

In numerous instances a city ticket office shared quarters with a freight sales office, or occasionally, with a passenger sales staff of a non-competitive railroad. In Omaha, the Milwaukee and the Missouri Pacific shared a passenger office; and in Vancouver, B. C., CM&StP shared quarters with a coastal steamship line.

Ticket offices were also a prime outlet for the sale of guided tours offered by American Express, Thomas Cook, and other firms. Tour companies often filled extra cars on regular trains and sometimes entire special trains, so the sale of tours at rail offices was a natural link. During the decades when overseas travel was by steamship, railroad city ticket offices frequently arranged such travel as well, a mutually beneficial circumstance since the international journey would begin aboard a passenger train.

With the emergence of air travel for business and overseas journeys, the need for city offices began to diminish, and most were phased out before 1960. Airline ticket offices and travel agencies, for the most part spawned by the air travel industry, now serve a similar purpose.

(Opposite page, left) In 1922, the window of the Milwaukee Road's newly opened office at 306 South Sixteenth Street in Omaha advertised the *Omaha-Chicago Limited* and the electrified route to Puget Sound. (Opposite page, right) Seven years later the road opened a new office at 1611 Farnam Street, and the *Arrow* was featured in the window. (Above) In October 1940 the Farnam Street office, by then shared with the Missouri Pacific, was modernized. MoPac advertised its new *Eagle*; Milwaukee Road still featured the *Arrow*, but the *Midwest Hiawatha* was less than two months away. — *Three photos, Milwaukee Road.*

DINING CARS

Today, when many airline flights are barely long enough to allow the cabin attendants to serve coffee, when food along the highways is largely the province of fast-food franchises, and when sit-down meals are found only on long-distance trains, it's difficult to appreciate how much attention the railroads gave to ensuring that passengers wouldn't miss a meal.

The Chicago, Milwaukee & St. Paul introduced dining cars on its Chicago-Minneapolis trains in 1882. In the ensuing four years, their use spread to two trains in each direction on both the Chicago-Twin Cities and the Chicago-Omaha routes, plus noon and early evening trains in both directions between Chicago and Milwaukee. These rolling restaurants were built by Harlan & Hollingsworth of Wilmington, Delaware. They were identified by letter rather than name or number. They were 70 feet long, rode on six-wheel trucks and, like all passenger cars of the time, had open platforms at each end. Even at the modest speeds of the era, it must have been an adventure for travelers, particularly women in long skirts, to reach the diner from elsewhere in the train.

The most common dining car configuration remained unchanged from the earliest dining cars until the Amtrak era. About a third of the car was devoted to kitchen, pantry, and supply areas, and a corridor along one side let passengers bypass them. The rest of the car was the dining room, with tables for four persons on one side, an off-center aisle, and tables for two on the opposite side. The earliest cars seated 30 at 5 pairs of tables, but by 1920 vestibules on diners had been omitted, creating space for a sixth pair of tables. The construction methods of the streamline era increased the inside width enough to allow four-place tables on both sides of the aisle. On trains with less demand for formal dining, food service facilities often occupied part of a car that also contained parlor seats, a lounge, or coach or sleeping accommodations.

At first the major domo of a car was known as a dining car conductor, but the title was later changed to steward. The steward seated the passengers; brought the menu and the meal check (on which the passengers wrote their order); then totaled the check, accepted payment, and made change. The steward often assisted the waiters by changing tablecloths and resetting the tables after the passengers at each table had finished. Waiters performed the same duties as waiters everywhere.

The diner crew had other duties not readily apparent to passengers. After the evening meal the steward and the chef had to determine what foodstuffs would be needed for the next day, to be obtained either at terminals or, in the case of the *Olympian*, the *Columbian*, and later the *Olympian Hiawatha*, at intermediate commissaries as well. Meanwhile, the two or three cooks and the three or four waiters would be busy washing dishes and cleaning the car. Only after these tasks were completed could they retire, either on improvised bunks in the diner itself or, after 1934, to a dormitory car elsewhere in the train. If the car spent the night in a major city, the railroad, at least in modern times, paid for lodging for the crew in a nearby hotel.

94

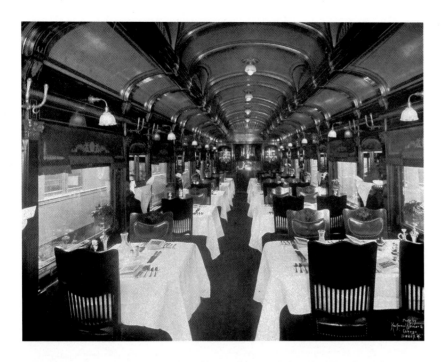

Mirrors in the pier panels between the windows and electric lights brightened the interior of this 1911 dining car, probably built for the all-steel *Olympian*. — *Milwaukee Road.*

Between Chicago and Milwaukee the 1927 edition of the *Pioneer Limited* carried a dining car named for Dan Healey, who had been steward of the train's dining car from 1899 to 1922. The Art Deco lamps between the windows and the slip covers on the chair backs relieved the somberness of the dark wood interior. — *Both photos, Milwaukee Road.*

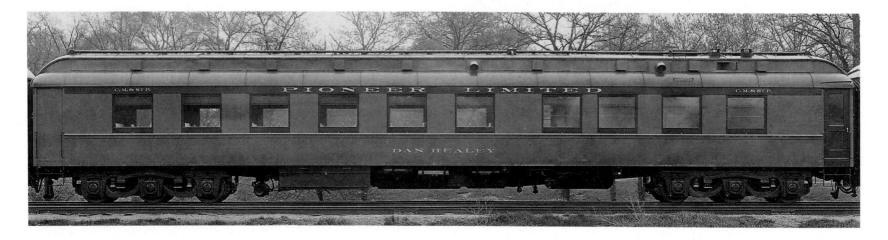

The second dining car *Dan Healey*, built by Pullman in 1931 and the last heavyweight diner acquired by the Milwaukee Road, reflected contemporary residential design trends, exemplified by the beamed ceiling, wall sconces, and wrought-iron chandeliers. At each end of the car was a pair of booths with wingback settees, foreshadowing a seating arrangement used years later in dining cars built for the *California Zephyr* and the *Panama Limited*. Ventilation grilles along the side of the clerestory indicate air conditioning, which was added to the car in 1934. — *Milwaukee Road*.

Milwaukee Road dining car service had several traditions. To announce the serving of meals, a waiter walked through the train playing several notes on a set of chimes. The road provided envelopes for guests desiring to mail menus to their friends. Particularly welcome on frigid northern-plains mornings was the immediate service of a complimentary demitasse of coffee to each breakfast guest. The Milwaukee road used a unique coffee cup, designed by William Dolphin of the dining car department about the beginning of the *Hiawatha* era. Inside the cup just below the top was a ring or lip, which virtually eliminated sloshing of hot beverages.

Milwaukee Road's dining car service expanded rapidly. By 1895, dining cars operated on trains 1 and 4, the predecessors of the *Pioneer Limited*; unnamed trains of the same numbers between Chicago and Omaha; and daytime trains 6 and 7 between Chicago and Watertown, Wisconsin. Lunch cars provided no-frills menus between Mason City, Iowa, and Canton, South Dakota, on Chicago-Mitchell, S. Dak., trains; and between Manilla and Sioux City, Iowa, on yet another pair of trains numbered 1 and 4 to and from Chicago. (Almost until the end of passenger train service, the Milwaukee Road was notorious for assigning identical numbers to more than one pair of trains — on different divisions, of course.)

Buffet-sleepers, some of them Pullman-operated, provided food service for first-class passengers between Chicago and Minneapolis via Savanna, Dubuque, and Austin; between Chicago and Michigan's upper peninsula; and between Minneapolis and St. Louis via the Iowa & Minnesota division to Mason City, Iowa, the Iowa Central Railroad to Hedrick, CM&StP again to Ottumwa, Iowa, and the Wabash to St. Louis.

Dining car operations became somewhat more complex by the first decade of the twentieth century. Chicago-Minneapolis, Chicago-Milwaukee, and Chicago-Omaha runs continued as before. Outlying portions of the system saw pairs of trains sharing a single dining car, switching it from one train to the other where the trains met. Buffet sleepers appeared on branchline runs to Ottuma, Iowa, and Fargo, North Dakota; other branches and short runs were served by cafe cars or buffet-parlor cars. A new style of car, the buffet-observation, graced the end of trains 56 and 3 between Minneapolis and La Crosse, Wisconsin, serving supper southbound and breakfast northbound. Such cars also made a two-stage westbound trip: Chicago to Marion, Iowa, on local train 9, continuing the next morning on the *China & Japan Fast Mail*, train 3, to Omaha, and returning to Chicago on the *Chicago Special*, train 4.

The Puget Sound Extension was completed in 1909. At first it offered only rudimentary passenger service. The first passenger trains carried dining cars only on the daytime segments of their trips or depended on station meal stops. First-quality twice-daily passenger service between Lake Michigan and

Rene Chaveaux was born in France, emigrated to Britain as a young man, and served as a chef for the London & North Eastern Railway. He later came to the United States and served the Milwaukee Road as a chef, then an instructor, and finally dining car inspector. He is pictured in his instructor's role at the Western Avenue commissary in Chicago. — *Milwaukee Road*. Adjacent are pictured the meal check, on which guests wrote their own orders, a blue-and-silver menu commemorating the twenty-fifth anniversary of the *Hiawatha*, and the cover of the dinner menu of the *Afternoon Hiawatha* of 1969.

Puget Sound began in May 1911 with the *Olympian* and the *Columbian*. Both carried dining cars the entire distance. Other additions to the road's food service that year were a full diner on Wisconsin Valley trains 1 and 2 between Wausau and Tomahawk, Wis., and a cafe-observation between Channing and Calumet, Mich., via McKeever and the Copper Range Railroad, to serve the north end of a sleeping car service from Chicago.

By the time America entered World War One, buffet-sleepers had been phased out, usually replaced by a more elaborate style of food-service vehicle. Library-buffet cars were introduced on the *Colorado Express* and cafe-library-observations on the *Colorado Special*. Regular diners began linking Madison, Wis., with both Milwaukee and Chicago.

From 1920 on, the road adjusted its dining car operations, trimming here, adding there, to fit traffic patterns and economic conditions.

In September 1922, the road's best-known steward died. Dan Healey had presided over the rituals of dinner from Chicago to Milwaukee and breakfast in the opposite direction on the daily round trip of his diner on trains 1 and 4, the *Pioneer Limited*, since 1899. Healey was the subject of newspaper columns and made hundreds of friends for the railway with his gracious hospitality and the efficiency with which he managed his car. At his death at age 69, he was reputedly the oldest dining car steward in the nation. The dining car of the re-equipped *Pioneer* of 1927 was named for him, and the honor was enhanced when "Dan Healey" was painted in gold upon the flanks of a new dining car constructed by Pullman in 1931. It was the last heavyweight diner acquired by the CMStP&P.

From fall 1928 to early 1933, the Milwaukee Road's dining car operation was supervised by eminent restaurateur George Rector, proprietor of a well-known New York restaurant (Rector's) and author of books and articles on culinary art. Rector organized a school in a special demonstration car at the

Dining-car kitchens were miracles of efficiency — they had to be. Four cooks, each with specific tasks, worked in the kitchen of a 48-seat diner (a 1937 streamlined car is shown). Between the kitchen and the dining room was the pantry, where china and silverware were stored, coffee was prepared, and waiters submitted and received their orders. Often a "pantry man" was stationed there full time to keep things flowing smoothly. — *Both photos, Milwaukee Road.*

Western Avenue Commissary in Chicago. He instructed the road's chefs in the fine points of food preparation, and his unique dishes were often added to the regular dining car menus.

Streamlined dining service arrived on the Milwaukee with the *Hiawatha* in May 1935. Cars 5251 and 5252 were lettered "Cafe," but the timetable described them as restaurant-buffet cars. The kitchen occupied the rear portion of the car. At the center was a dining room with six tables for four persons each. The windowless forward third of the car contained a bar across the entire width of the front of the car (which meant the car had to be at the head of the train) and an accompanying lounge. In 1942 they were rebuilt as mid-train tap-diners for the *Midwest Hiawatha*.

The next year, a pair of 48-seat diners emerged from Milwaukee Shops for the second set of *Hiawathas*, and in 1937 seven more identical cars were built for the *Olympian*. In 1938 four new diners rolled out of the shops for the third edition of the *Afternoon Hiawatha* and the new *Morning Hiawatha*. Prewar additions to the dining car roster ended with a pair of cars for the *Afternoon Hi* of 1942.

World War Two brought to the Milwaukee's dining cars maximum patronage, long waiting lines at mealtime, and extended serving hours. Special military train movements and operation of the *Olympian* in two sections much of the time meant constant operation of every dining car and no rest days for their crews.

Peacetime brought optimism about the future of passenger travel, and additional diners were an important part of the road's car-building program in the late 1940s. The first diners, a group of six, were for the *Olympian Hiawatha* of 1947, and six more followed the next year for the *Afternoon*, *Chippewa*, and *Morning Hiawathas*. They were all 48-seat cars except those for the *Olympian Hiawatha*, which were built as 40-seaters but subsequently were changed to 48-seat cars. A dozen diner-lounges, lunch-lounges, and tap-diners were built in 1947 and 1948 for the *Midwest*, *Olympian*, and *Afternoon Hiawathas*, and the *Pioneer Limited*. They had lunch, dining, and tavern or tap rooms of varying configurations, depending on their intended assignment. For example, the cars assigned to the *Midwest Hiawatha* needed less tavern space than others since parts of Iowa were dry and the state was entirely dry on Sundays.

The final streamlined dining cars were a group of six parlor-diners named for on-line towns having "Grove" as the second word of their name — Elm Grove and Morton Grove, for example. The *Grove* cars seated 24 passengers at six 4-place tables and had 16 parlor (first class) seats. The cars were assigned to secondary trains such as locals 10 and 19 between Green Bay, Wis., and Chicago.

The dining rooms of the 1938 *Hiawatha* diners were partitioned by drapes into three areas with four tables each. The arrow motif in the fabric was a subtle reminder of the train's namesake, who could outrun the arrows he had shot from his bow. The use of placemats on the tables in place of the more usual tablecloths was a short-lived experiment. A steward and two waiters are shown at work. The corridor beyond the steward makes a jog to the right past the pantry and the kitchen. — *Milwaukee Road.*

The diners built in 1948 for the *Midwest Hiawatha* had a short tavern section (shown here set up for breakfast). Drinks were prepared by the steward in a work station at the end of the car, just visible beyond the bulkhead. The stainless steel pillars and planters echoed the decorative treatment used in the Skytop parlor cars. — *Milwaukee Road*.

OBSERVATION CARS

By the turn of the century the passenger train had come of age. Open platforms, which made passing between cars uncomfortable in inclement weather and dangerous at any time, were giving way to enclosed vestibules. Flexible canvas devices known as diaphragms formed a passageway protected from the weather between the vestibules of adjacent cars. The train could be considered an integral unit rather than a loosely connected group of cars. This increased the popularity of dining cars and played a part in the creation of the special cars attached to the rear of the limited trains.

For these observation cars, the open platform of the non-vestibule car was given a floor the full width of the car and deep enough to hold two rows of folding chairs. A decorative railing around the platform provided a measure of safety. The car roof was extended the full depth of the platform, and the rear wall or bulkhead of the car was set back a few feet between the sides, forming an area protected from the wind. Platform riders were protected from the bright sun and not-so-bright soot and cinders by an awning around the edges of the roof.

Access to the observation platform was from a door at the rear of the car. Early cars generally had the door at one side with a king-size picture window; on later cars, the door was placed in the center with windows on each side. Observation cars offered an excellent view of the passing scenery, and they exuded a certain amount of snob appeal, since they were usually reserved for sleeping and parlor car passengers.

The Milwaukee Road featured open-platform observation cars through the 1927 editions of the *Olympian* and the *Pioneer* Limited. Observation cars with an enclosed sun room, or solarium, better suited to high speeds and free of the nuisances of cinders and dust, were introduced shortly thereafter on the *Pioneer* and the *Arrow*. Full-length lounge cars with observation platforms were used on the *Olympian* until World War Two, and they were also assigned to the *Arrow* and its forerunner, the *Omaha-Chicago Limited*. When CM&StP participated in operation of the *Overland Limited* in the early 1900s, it carried observation cars. The *Southwest Limited, Pacific Limited, Columbian*, and nameless trains 6 and 11 between Chicago and Sioux City, Iowa, all carried observation-sleeping cars of various configurations.

Early in the century the *Pioneer Limited* carried observation-parlor cars, and such cars were also found in the consists of the *National Park Limited*, the *On Wisconsin*, the *Day Express* between Chicago and the Twin Cities, trains 55 and 56 between La Crosse, Wisconsin, and Minneapolis, and locals 33, 34, 35, and 36 between Des Moines and Spirit Lake, Iowa. Some of these cars offered buffet service, and assignments varied from time to time.

Several trains carried cafe-observation cars, which offered a more extensive menu than the buffet. These were used where there was insufficient demand for food service to warrant a full diner. Cafe-observations were the most widely used type of observation car on the railway, operating even on lines which saw no sleeping, parlor, or full dining car service. Cafe cars ran not

This obviously posed photo — rarely did passengers exclaim over the wonders of Chicago's Western Avenue coach yard — illustrates the details of the rear end of an observation car (this is *City of Everett*): polished brass railing supported by black ironwork, markers on the corners of the body, floodlight overhead to illuminate the canyons of the Rockies after dark, and the drumhead sign telling all that this is the *Olympian*. Note that the platform can be used for boarding and detraining only on the right side of the car, and that was primarily a convenience for the flagman. — *Milwaukee Road.*

103

The last open-platform observation cars of the *Pioneer Limited* were those of the 1927 train, built and operated by Pullman. The car is shown during exhibition in Milwaukee. — *Milwaukee Road.*

Smokeless travel on the *Olympian* meant more than bipolars and quills up front — note the admonition against smoking posted above the rear window of this car, which appears to be one built for the original *Olympian*. The observation room occupied the rear third of the car; forward were a smoking compartment, ladies' lounge, barber shop, baths, and soda fountain. — *Two photos, Milwaukee Road: Asahel Curtis.*

In 1924 there was no finer way to view Washington's Cascade Mountains than from the full-length observation car of the *Olympian*. Later the train received a faster schedule, which put it through the Cascades at night, but passengers then had a daytime view of Adair Loop in the Bitterroots east of Avery, Idaho. The open cars made their final trips September 12, 1941, the end of the summer tourist season. During World War Two they were enclosed and used to carry company materials. — *Milwaukee Road: Asahel Curtis.*

(Above, right) The *Arrow* of 1926 featured limousine lounge cars *Maquoketa* and *Waucoma*, both rebuilt from buffet-observation cars. (Above) In the enclosed solarium, which replaced the observation platform, passengers could open and close the windows with cranks like those used in automobiles. (Opposite page) The telephone was connected while passengers boarded the train at Omaha and Chicago. — *Three photos, Milwaukee Road.*

only on the Chicago-Twin Cities and Chicago-Omaha main lines but also on such diverse trains as the *Northern Michigan Special*, the *Sioux*, trains 115 and 116 between Harlowton and Great Falls, Montana, and on an interline movement via CM&StP subsidiary Tacoma Eastern and Union Pacific between Seattle and Hoquiam, Washington. Cafe-observations were eventually either replaced by enclosed solarium cars or converted to that style.

To afford sleeping car passengers a grand view of the scenic splendors of the Cascades, Bitterroots, and Rockies, mountain observation cars were operated on the *Olympian* and *Columbian* during warm months. Rebuilt from wood cars, they had waist-high sides and thin posts supporting a roof. The spartan interior contained wood seats in facing pairs on each side of the aisle. Glass partitions between groups of seats afforded protection from chilly mountain air.

107

It is obviously a chilly day in 1939 as the *Olympian*'s passengers view Montana or Sixteen Mile Canyon from an open observation car. The canyon is reputed to have some of the best trout streams in Montana; it is also known for rattlesnakes, which like to nestle against the rails on sunny days. — *Milwaukee Road*.

The Super Domes could be considered successors to the open mountain observation cars — and also predecessors of Amtrak's Superliner lounges. Because the seats were low and the view ahead was restricted, Milwaukee's domes weren't as popular with passengers as other roads' dome cars.
— *Jim Scribbins*.

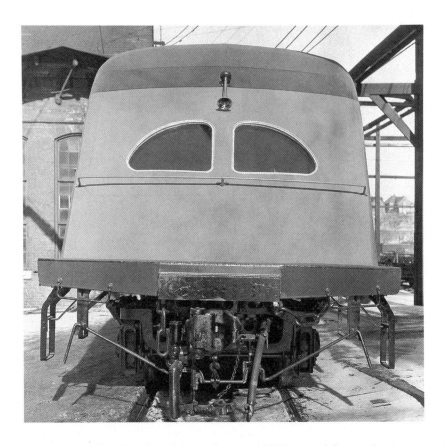

Standing outside Milwaukee Shops in January 1935 is one of the two Beaver Tail parlor cars intended for a train that didn't yet have a name. By the time the cars entered service, though, brass "Hiawatha" script appeared in a maroon rectangle below the windows, the maroon letterboard stripe had been redesigned to dip beneath the air horn (used when the train was backing), and the roof had been repainted silver. — *Milwaukee Road.*

Beaver Tails *Omeme* and *Opeche* entered service in the fall of 1936. Four windows replaced the two windows of the first Beaver Tail cars, but the couch inside faced forward. In 1942 the cars were restyled to be much like the 1939 Beaver Tails. — *Milwaukee Road.*

The cars were introduced about 1920 and for the most part were confined to the electrified divisions of the road, although for a while they ventured into oil-burning steam engine territory as far west as St. Maries, Idaho, on the *Columbian.* The electrification prolonged the life of these cars after most other roads had discontinued theirs, but the 1941 season was their last. They were not restored to service after the war.

Less than a decade later, a mid-century version of the mountain observa-

tion car appeared on the *Olympian, Afternoon,* and *Morning Hiawathas*: the Super Dome. Domes were first placed in regular service in 1947 on Burlington's *Twin Zephyrs,* direct competitors of the *Hiawathas.* It was some five years before the *Hiawathas* received domes, the first full-length domes in railroading. They were built by Pullman-Standard and delivered at Christmas 1952. The dome itself was nearly 80 feet long and had 625 square feet of glass, necessitating a 16-ton-capacity air conditioning system. Special six-

The third and last version of the Beaver Tail parlor car was a true observation car, with a rear-facing sofa and enormous windows shaded by fins. Milwaukee Shops craftsmanship extended to such details as the wood fins which diffused the glare of the lights in the underside of the luggage racks. — *Milwaukee Road.*

wheel trucks were designed to support the heavy cars. Sixty-eight persons could be seated in the dome, which, unfortunately, didn't provide as good a view as the Burlington's shorter domes. A cafe-lounge was located below the center of the dome, but even modest meal service was impractical and the room was soon used only as a cocktail lounge. The Super Domes replaced the tap-lounges of the *Hiawathas*; those cars were eventually assigned to secondary trains.

Beaver Tail parlor cars were practically a trademark of the *Hiawathas*. No other railroad had anything quite like them, although a pair of carriages on Britain's London & North Eastern Railway bore a strong resemblance to those of the original *Hi.* Those first Beaver Tails, named *Nokomis* and *Wenonah*, had small rear windows, but it really didn't matter since the rear seats faced forward and couldn't be turned. *Omeme* and *Opeche* of the 1937 train had

larger windows and more of them, but the couch at the rear of the car also faced forward. It took the expertise of industrial designer Otto Kuhler to turn the couch around and provide great expanses of glass through which to observe the track receding at 100 mph. Silver-colored fins attached to the sloping rear surface provided shade — and a stunning identification of the *Twin Cities Hiawatha.* In recognition of Kuhler's design a small plate reading "Styled by Otto Kuhler" was affixed to the rear of each of the four Beaver Tails of 1939 *Hiawathas.* (Such tribute is rare in railroading.)

For the final version of the *Hiawatha* in 1948, industrial designer Brooks Stevens created the Skytop Lounge, described as "the finishing touch to a perfect train." It continued the tradition of distinctively styled Milwaukee Road solariums. The Skytops were considered the most strikingly contoured solarium cars in North America.

For its first 18 months of operation, the *Olympian Hiawatha* carried standard Pullman compartment-drawing room-observation cars, substituting for the Skytop sleeper-observations, which were still under construction. The cars offered the fastest observation-platform ride anywhere, since 90- to 100-mph running was the norm between Chicago and La Crosse, Wisconsin. — *Jim Scribbins*.

(Opposite page) The 1948 *Morning* and *Afternoon Hiawathas* received the last observation cars built by Milwaukee Shops, the Skytop parlor-observation cars. The curved sofa around the perimeter of the solarium was intended for sociability, not for viewing. The *Olympian Hiawatha* carried similar-looking Skytop sleeper-observations built by Pullman-Standard. — *Milwaukee Road*.

The blizzard of January 29, 1947, is still remembered in Milwaukee. One of the first trains to move after the storm was a double-headed extra passenger train to Seattle. Snow shovelers at the west end of the Milwaukee station pay scant attention to the Hudsons, one conventional and one shrouded, just sent down from the shops freshly coaled and watered. — *Milwaukee Journal photo; Milwaukee Road collection.*

WINTER

A long the Milwaukee Road cold weather was the norm for at least one-third of the year. In much of the territory that was served by the road, temperatures rarely rise above freezing from Thanksgiving to early April. Extreme cold could be expected anywhere but west of the Cascades; even Missouri and southern Indiana could produce below-zero cold.

Along with the cold came snow. Usually the road took snow in stride, but some years were memorable. Near Chicago, trains were frequent enough to keep lines open just by their passage, but switch heaters were a standard item in terminals and yards. Snow created problems in addition to its accumulation. Inevitably, some motorist would slide off a snowy grade crossing to block one or more tracks during the commuter rush.

Across the prairie of northern Illinois, winds made snowplow service a more frequent entry on the dispatcher's train sheet than farther north in Wisconsin, and from the Twin Cities west to the Rockies, wind created major problems. Not only could wind-blown snow quickly engulf every wheel of a stopped train, but wind could blow fine snow into the electrical apparatus of diesel locomotives, creating short circuits that brought the locomotives to a standstill. Cold alone could freeze idling diesel locomotives.

Cold, wind, and snow could usually win a battle with the Milwaukee Road, though the railroad would eventually win the war (and without waiting to enlist the resources of May and June).

Severe cold was not a problem in the Cascade Range, but that area receives the heaviest snowfall in the 48 contiguous states. The first year the Puget Sound Extension was in service, as much as 46 feet of snow accumulated on the level in that area. Rotary snowplows encountered slides 20 to 40 feet deep, and on occasion they and the locomotives pushing them were buried by snowslides. The customary snowplow train in steam days was a rotary pointed forward, a 2-6-6-2 for propulsion, and another rotary facing the rear. The arrangement provided for clearing snow in either direction and reduced the likelihood of being trapped.

The railroad began building snowsheds in Snoqualmie Pass in 1911, and the opening of Snoqualmie Tunnel in 1915 alleviated the problem somewhat. Electrification made winter more bearable, because electric locomotives are more efficient at lower temperatures, unlike steam locomotives. The railroad added electrically operated rotary plows to its arsenal.

In January and February 1936, the railroad had to bring rotary plows from South Dakota to Milwaukee to clear drifted snow that was beyond the capabilities of its wedge plows. One morning conditions were so severe that the southbound *Fast Mail* and *Copper Country Limited*, already far behind schedule, stalled near Sturtevant, 23 miles south of Milwaukee. At Lake, 7 miles south of Milwaukee, a rotary plow was switched to the northbound track to pass the stalled trains. Behind the rotary was the Chicago-bound *Pioneer Limited*, which rescued the passengers of the two stalled trains.

The Milwaukee's last major battle with snow on its line to the West Coast was early in 1978, when severe cold and wind-driven snow closed all the road's branch lines in North and South Dakota.

115

Rotary 900207, built by American Locomotive Company's Cooke works, was brought from the Dakotas to eastern Wisconsin to fight the storms of early 1936. — *Milwaukee Road: Harvey Uecker.*

The craftsmen of Milwaukee Shops constructed this wedge plow in 1939. Its hydraulically operated side wings obviated the need to follow the plow with a cut widener. The 40-ton machine was controlled by an operator viewing its progress from the cupola. — *Milwaukee Road*.

In the 1950s John P. Kiley, president of the road, suggested that tenders from scrapped steam locomotives could be converted to wedge plows. The conversion was done at the shops at Miles City, Montana, where some of the personnel posed with the latest example of their craftsmanship. Looking on is 4-8-4 No. 209, wondering if the same will happen to its tender. — *Milwaukee Road*.

117

118

Electric rotary X900212 was brought east from the Cascades to South Dakota in March 1966 to help clean up after a blizzard. It is shown being pushed and powered by four GP9s near Lemmon, digging out a drift that has already been loosened with dynamite. A few miles west, near McIntosh, crews pause to consider their tactics. — *Three photos, Milwaukee Road.*

Electric rotary X900212 is shown being pushed and powered by GP9 No. 324 at Avery, Idaho, January 1, 1969. The machine can also draw current to turn the blade (but not to propel itself) from the overhead wire. The inefficiency of steam power in cold weather prompted the development of the electric rotary snowplows. — *Milwaukee Road: Wade Stevenson.*

STEAM FREIGHT TRAINS

By the turn of the century, 4-6-0 locomotives were the prime movers of freight traffic on CM&StP. The wheel arrangement was well suited to the profiles and the commodities of the St. Paul. Ten-Wheelers remained relatively plentiful on the road until dieselization.

The road's first eight-coupled locomotives were Consolidations built by Baldwin in 1901. They were followed quickly by 20 built at Milwaukee Shops. Larger 2-8-0s were built in bigger batches during the next few years, and the road's most muscular C-class engines came with the acquisition of the Chicago, Terre Haute & Southeastern in 1921.

When the Puget Sound Extension was opened the road sought to move unbroken trains the entire distance between the West Coast and Chicago, mandating more modern power. While 4-6-0s continued to hold forth between St. Paul and Chicago, the road chose the Prairie type (2-6-2) for the territory between the Twin Cities and the Rockies, and the Mikado (2-8-2), a relatively new type, to handle freight across the five mountain ranges between central Montana and the West Coast. Both were designed to burn lignite coal from the railway's mines at Roundup, Mont., the source of fuel for all coal-burning locomotives west of the Twin Cities.

The class L1 2-8-2s were considered a successful design, and eventually the road had more 2-8-2s than any other wheel arrangement. Subsequent class L2 engines were built at the shops in Milwaukee, by the Brooks and Schenectady works of American Locomotive Company, and by the Baldwin Locomotive Works. Class L2 was so popular that its construction continued even after the arrival of 100 heavy Mikados built to the standard design of the United States Railroad Administration.

It became evident almost immediately that the L1 engines were strained to their utmost on mountain grades. Snoqualmie Pass in the Cascades, for instance, had stretches as steep as 2.7 percent. The road acquired 36 class N Mallets. These Alco 2-6-6-2s were the Milwaukee's only articulateds, and they were put to work as helpers in what soon would become the domain of electric locomotives.

The final phase of steam freight locomotive design on CMStP&P was the introduction of the 4-8-4, the Northern type, in 1930. Engine 9700, sometimes known as "Orphan Annie," was a stretched class F6 Hudson. Its first assignment was in passenger service between Minneapolis and Harlowton, Mont., opposite one of the 4-6-4s. Next, it worked on Lines East freight trains before finally settling down on the Idaho division between Avery, Idaho, and Othello, Washington.

Seven years later the use of the 4-8-4 wheel arrangement began in earnest on the Milwaukee with the arrival of thirty class S2 locomotives. Engines 200-229 moved heavier trains faster between Bensenville and Council Bluffs and between Bensenville and Harlowton, reason enough to order 10 more such machines, which were delivered in 1940.

Ten S3s arrived during 1944, although the road would have preferred

120

Chicago, Terre Haute & Southeastern 4-6-0 No. 2239 is switching near Bedford, Indiana. The Ten-Wheeler was built for the Southern Indiana by Rogers in 1899 and retired in 1934. — *Milwaukee Road.*

more Electro-Motive FT diesels. Engines 260-269 were hybrid designs — what modelers call kit-bashed — a Delaware & Hudson boiler on a Rock Island frame, with a Union Pacific tender behind.

There was yet another 4-8-4. As the S2s were arriving in 1938, Milwaukee Shops, as a "make-work" project, put together a second S1, No. 251, principally with parts from Baldwin and its suppliers. Intended from the start for use between the electric zones, it was built as an oil-burner, and it was a twin to No. 9700, which had been renumbered 250. The S1s and S3s had nearly identical tractive effort and were equally adept in freight and passenger service.

The railroad was reorganized as the Chicago, Milwaukee, St. Paul & Pacific in mid-January 1928 and began to establish plans for an efficient network of through, or "time," freight trains, which would move across a subdi-

vision without picking up or setting out cars. Within a few months the general manager's office directed all operating officers to schedule a sufficient fleet of daily time freights to ensure expeditious handling of all loaded cars, giving particular attention to livestock and perishable items.

Livestock, desirably, was to move in entire trains, much as today's unit trains now haul coal and grain. When stock movements were sparse, other time-sensitive freight was to accompany the animals in order to create decent-sized trains. When practicable, trains were to be made up to the maximum tonnage rating of the locomotive assigned. Division officers were to exercise their judgment about whether to operate a second section.

The *Freight Train Manual* provided detailed instructions for routing cars. For example, cars from Racine, Wisconsin, to stations on the Iowa & Minnesota Division between St. Paul and Faribault, Minn., were sent via Milwau-

The Superior Division patrol from the north, scheduled in the timetable and thus not displaying white flags, is almost to Milwaukee's Bluemound Yard as it crosses the Menomonee River just north of Grand Avenue tower in August 1949. Motive power is a relatively modern class C5 Consolidation built by Milwaukee Shops in 1913 — and retired two years after the photo was taken. — *Jim Scribbins.*

Train 68 arrives Calmar, Iowa, from Mason City in December 1952 with 2-8-2 No. 466 on the head end. Calmar was in the middle of the Marquette-Mason City line of the Iowa & Dakota Division and at the end of a line from Austin and the Twin Cities. Additionally, an Iowa Division branch from Oxford Junction joined the I&D a few miles west of Calmar at Jackson Junction. — *Don L. Hofsommer*.

USRA heavy Mikado No. 325 moves a train carrying a substantial number of refrigerator cars over the C&M in 1944. — *Milwaukee Road.*

A Challenger or a Yellowstone would have been proud of the massive tenders that were given to the Milwaukee's 2-6-6-2s when they were rebuilt from compound to simple locomotives. Class N3 No. 58 is shown on a timber trestle on the branch to Metaline Falls in 1950. Dieselization would come a year later. — *Phillip R. Hastings.*

125

The outer end of the St. Maries-Elk River line in Idaho required 2-6-6-2s, but over the rest of the branch trains could be handled easily by 2-8-0s. Motive power was changed at Clarkia. Note that both engines on this line through heavily forested country are oil burners. — *Phillip R. Hastings.*

The Pend Oreille River valley north of Newport, Washington, reminded the photographer of the Connecticut River valley of his boyhood, and the Coffin feedwater heater and inboard-bearing trailer of the 2-6-6-2 brought back memories of the same appliances on Boston & Maine 2-10-2s. — *Phillip R. Hastings.*

126

Train 83 was a Bensenville-St. Paul time freight which followed the *Morning Hi* west out of Milwaukee. On June 30, 1949, it approaches the Soo Line crossing at Duplainville, with S2 No. 221 and 97 cars. — *Jim Scribbins*.

(Opposite page) Number 9700, the road's first 4-8-4, was an appendage to the first group of Hudsons and shared many components with them. The orphan S1 was eventually converted to oil firing and assigned to the gap between the two electrified zones. — *Milwaukee Road*.

kee and St. Paul, while to stations between Faribault and Conover, Iowa, they were routed via Savanna, Marquette, and Calmar. Cars from Mobridge, South Dakota, to stations between Waukesha and Lima Center, Wis., were routed via Milwaukee; to Madison, Wis., via Portage, Wis.; and to all other Prairie du Chien Division stations via St. Paul, River Junction, Minn. (opposite La Crosse, Wis.), and Marquette, Iowa.

Trains 263 and 264 between Lake Michigan and Puget Sound were probably the Milwaukee's best-known freight trains of the steam era. Other important time freights of 1940 were 62 and 63 between Sioux Falls, Mason City and Savanna (where they consolidated with Illinois division trains to and from Bensenville); 61 and 68 between Bensenville and Council Bluffs; 65 and 70 linking Milwaukee and Kansas City; and 69 and 74 between Chicago

Class S3 4-8-4 No. 263 takes a time freight across the Chicago & North Western's main line at Tama, Iowa, in 1947. This was reputed to be the only crossing of double-track main lines in Iowa. — *Henry J. McCord.*

and the upper peninsula of Michigan. Train 69 began its trek from Galewood Yard on the west side of Chicago rather than from Bensenville, and 74 terminated at Western Avenue Yard, across the main tracks from the CMStP&P coach yard.

Time freights serving Madison, Wis., included 163 and 166 between Bensenville and Madison via Janesville; and trains 63 and 68 between Milwaukee and Madison over the the road's original route (the Milwaukee & Mississippi).

In 1940 there were no Kansas City-St. Paul trains, but two trains in each direction between Davenport's Nahant Yard and River Junction, Minn., linked Kansas City division trains with Bensenville-St. Paul time freights. The Nahant-River Junction trains were unique in that they changed timetable direction and train number at Samoa, Iowa, across the Mississippi from Savanna, Ill. For example, 88 eastbound from Nahant became westbound 89 at Samoa, and 76 from River Junction changed its identity to 67 as it passed the junction at the west edge of Sabula, Iowa.

The *Freight Train Manual* covered consist and connections only, making no reference to operating stops, such as water and coal stops, stops for crew changes, and stops to attach and detach the helper that was usually required to climb Elgin Hill out of the Fox River valley. The *Manual* was an adjunct to the timetable to assist dispatchers and road and yard supervisors. The work

Ten-Wheeler 1029 emerges from the enginehouse at Bozeman, Montana, to take a train to Gallatin Gateway over what was originally the Gallatin Valley Electric Railway, whose sole interurban car shared track with the steam trains of its owner. — *David Plowden.*

(Opposite page) The North Lake patrol (Milwaukee Road lingo for local or way freight) leaves Menomonee Falls for the west end of the branch on a midsummer day in 1954. The most modern details on the 2-6-2 are the 1940s number glasses flanking the headlight and the steel classification flags. Now the far end of the branch has become a tourist railroad, the station is the property of the local historical society, and Milwaukee's suburbs extend well beyond once-rural Menomonee Falls. — *Jim Scribbins.*

outlined in the 1940 *Freight Train Manual* for two time freights, 63 and 75, illustrates the detail and coordination necessary to establish adequate freight train service.

First let's follow train 63, which ran from Chicago to Council Bluffs. It included cars received directly from Terre Haute Division 67, from transfer runs from Galewood and Western Avenue yards, and from the Indiana Harbor Belt before its 10:30 a.m. departure from Bensenville. Its duties included forwarding cars to connecting lines at Council Bluffs; handling Kansas City, Sioux City and Des Moines cars; and forwarding traffic for the Dubuque line and stations beyond Marquette on the Iowa & Dakota and Iowa & Southern Minnesota divisions. Those cars were taken from Savanna by another 63 in Milwaukee's bewildering numbering scheme. If tonnage was light at Bensenville, 63 could accept cars for other principal stations along the Iowa Division.

Train 63's first work along the way was to set out Kansas City cars at Lanark, Ill., where Milwaukee-Kansas City time freight 75 was waiting. Then at Savanna No. 63 made a longer stop to switch out cars for Sioux Falls 63 and to pick up cars from Milwaukee, Rockford, and Freeport, Ill. Across the Mississippi at Samoa, train 63 added cars from train 78 from Dubuque and

Mikado 522 has just crossed the Chicago Great Western at Holcomb and is heading south toward Ladd, Ill, in August 1947. The engineer has the door in front of him open for air. — *Jim Scribbins*.

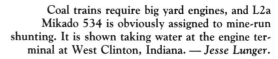

Coal trains require big yard engines, and L2a Mikado 534 is obviously assigned to mine-run shunting. It is shown taking water at the engine terminal at West Clinton, Indiana. — *Jesse Lunger*.

A transfer freight from the Chestnut Street line (better known as the Beer line) approaches the joint Northern and Superior Divisions main line at North Milwaukee in April 1948. Number 713 was built in 1912 for mountain service. — *Jim Scribbins*.

Rolling east at Perry, Iowa, is one of Milwaukee Road's final group of 4-8-4s. Because the War Production Board had placed restrictions on the creation of new locomotive designs, the S3 combined existing designs of three railroads: It was essentially a Rock Island R67-class 4-8-4, but the boiler echoed the clean lines of Delaware & Hudson's copy of the R67; the tender was based on a Union Pacific design. — *Henry J. McCord.*

Extra 233 West ducks beneath the Chicago & North Western's freight belt at the west edge of Wauwatosa, Wisconsin, in July 1946. Four Pennsy automobile box cars are behind the 4-8-4's tender. — *Jim Scribbins.*

An L3 2-8-2 leaves the lower yard at Marquette, Iowa, for Dubuque in 1952. Atop its smokebox front is a red gyrating warning light, illuminated automatically during an emergency brake application. Several classes of Milwaukee locomotives were built with the bell mounted off-center. — *Cecil Cook.*

Three Mikados team up to move a freight around St. Paul Union Depot and up the grade through the west side of the city. The small coal bunker of the tender of the third member of the trip indicates demotion to yard duty. — *Both photos, Ron Nixon.*

It's high noon at the Hastings & Dakota Division crew-change point of Montevideo, Minnesota. The westbound *Columbian*'s F6a Hudson is being groomed while a 1912 Brooks 2-8-2 does some local switching. — *Ernest A. Lehmann*.

La Crosse, and train 178 from Davenport (Nahant). (Remember, trains paralleling the Mississippi changed number and direction at Samoa.)

At Marion, Iowa, cars for Cedar Rapids were set out and any "hot" cars for western Iowa were added behind the tender of the S2. At Pickering, priority cars were received from the Minneapolis & St. Louis. A pause at Madrid found 63 exchanging cars with trains 168 and 169, a turnaround train serving Des Moines.

Midnight found 63 in Perry, Iowa, leaving cars for train 363, which ran up the branch through Rockwell City to Spencer, Iowa. At Manilla, Sioux City cars were detached to become a train of their own (yet another train 63), then the time freight completed its run at Council Bluffs at 5 a.m. Cars for the Union Pacific would be delivered by 7:30; deliveries to other railroads would be a bit later that morning.

Let's follow a Milwaukee-Kansas City train — No. 75, the train which connected with Chicago-Council Bluffs 63 at Lanark in the previous example.

One of two time freights linking Milwaukee with Kansas City, 75 was on the road at 4 a.m. heading toward Chicago from Milwaukee's Air Line Yard after receiving cars from Green Bay and Oshkosh. Train 75's mission was to move cars to Kansas City, Iowa points, Freeport, Ill., and Beloit, Wis., in that order of importance.

At Sturtevant, No. 75 left the double-track First District of the Milwaukee Division, paused to pick up cars brought out from Racine on train 165, and entered the Second District, the former Racine & Southwestern Division. In addition, the train had a change in identity and direction — the first 23 miles of its trip had been eastbound as train 750 (eastbound according to timetable, but south by the compass). At Beloit cars were set out for that city and for the line to Rockford and Ladd, Ill.; cars from those points filled out No. 75. Freeport benefited from a set-out, and the next stop was at Lanark to drop cars for points along the Council Bluffs main line and receive cars brought from Bensenville on time freight 63.

Mikados 626 and 651 work together pulling train 164 south over the former Northern Montana Division at Glengarry, Mont., near Lewistown, on St. Patrick's Day 1946. — *Warren R. McGee.*

Train 95 is westbound at Maynard on Washington's beautiful Olympic Peninsula on July 21, 1953. Behind 2-8-0 No. 1232 are empty box cars to be filled with wood products. — *John C. Illman.*

A caboose that has escaped the company's rebuilding program brings up the rear of a train on the Joliet Branch, the former Chicago, Milwaukee & Gary, at Momence, Illinois. In the arms of the woman on the rear platform is an exception to the note that appeared next to so many trains in the public timetable, "Will not carry checked baggage or dogs." — *A. C. Kalmbach.*

Train 75 took on another number as it entered the Dubuque & Illinois Division at Kittredge: It became train 175 (all Southwestern trains prefixed their numbers with a 1) and kept that number as far as Davenport's Nahant Yard to avoid conflict with schedule numbers from Bensenville.

In 1940, Milwaukee-Kansas City trains operated via the Ashdale cutoff along the east side of the Mississippi, bypassing Savanna. At East Moline, Ill., the train set out Quad Cities traffic, then crossed the Mississippi into Iowa on Davenport, Rock Island & Northwestern's Crescent Bridge. At Davenport, cars for local points on the Kansas City Division were set out for train 79, which would follow 75 all the way to Kansas City, and cars from Iowa Division 75 from Dubuque and La Crosse became part of the hotshot.

Train 75 headed into the sunset, pausing late in the evening at Ottumwa to add cars brought from Cedar Rapids by yet another train 175. At Laredo, Missouri, 75 picked up cars according to the dispatcher's instructions, then made a straight shot across the final subdivision and over the road's original Missouri River bridge to Kansas City's Suburban Junction. There No. 75 dropped a block of cars for Kansas City Southern 41, due out two hours later, and finally tied up a few minutes later at 6:15 a.m. at Coburg Yard.

Train 75 made close connections to departing freights of all the railroads to the west and south. The closest connection was to the Santa Fe, with a train leaving at 8, and the final delivery was to the Katy for a 10:30 a.m. departure. Between those were departures of freights of the Missouri Pacific, the St. Louis-San Francisco, the Union Pacific, and the Rock Island.

The Milwaukee Road's last steam power, 4-8-4s 260-269, were delivered at the same time as its largest group of FTs, engines 42-47. For about a decade, modern steam and new diesels could be found working together, sharing time freight duties. In fact, every type of steam freight locomotive owned by CMStP&P was working until the final act. The class G8 4-6-0s that had been rebuilt from turn-of-the-century Baldwin class B4s remained intact until 1956, when the youngest of them were 50 years of age. In part, their endurance demonstrated the versatility of the "Geeps" of their era, but it also recognizes that much of the Milwaukee route structure was made up of anachronistic rural branches. The final steam run on the Milwaukee Road was not made by a Northern or a streamlined Hudson but by G8 1004.

Mikados 626 and 651 have 33 loads and 5 empties totaling 2475 tons behind them on the Northern Montana line, on March 17, 1946. — *Warren R. McGee.*

ELECTRIC FREIGHT TRAINS

The Puget Sound Extension of the Chicago, Milwaukee & St. Paul, nearly 1400 route miles, linked the Missouri River, midway across South Dakota, with the body of water for which the extension was named. Traffic did not meet expectations from the start. The Great Northern and the Northern Pacific were already established in the route's sparsely settled territory, and Milwaukee's line was within sight of NP's route across much of Montana and Washington. Five years after completion of the Mobridge-Tacoma extension, the Panama Canal opened, giving Pacific shipping direct access to the East Coast of the U. S. The Milwaukee Road's need to reduce operating costs and improve train efficiency was clearly evident.

The road had five mountain ranges to cross: the Belts, Rockies, and Bitterroots in Montana and Idaho, and the Saddles and Cascades in Washington. Freights had to be triple-headed, requiring an inordinate amount of manpower, coal, and water — and the trains moved at a snail's pace. The road's new 2-6-6-2s offered some improvement, but in severe winter weather they could pull little more than the 2-8-2s.

Another complication arose from a massive forest fire in the Bitterroots in 1910. The conflagration could not be attributed to any railroad's locomotives, but it nonetheless brought legislation requiring use of oil-burning engines in the area. Fuel oil was more expensive than coal, and it had to be brought in from far away.

In the mountains, however, there was an abundance of waterpower which could be harnessed to generate electricity. Two short but heavy-duty electrification projects were already operating in the region. Great Northern energized its first Cascade Tunnel in Washington in 1909; and Butte, Anaconda & Pacific electrified its line between Butte and Anaconda, Mont., four years later. Both were unquestionably successful. The BA&P carried heavy tonnage over steep grades. Though it was a mining railroad, it had a run of sufficient distance to be considered a road-haul. The BA&P particularly influenced the Milwaukee's choice of electrification system.

The Milwaukee had considered electrification in the Bitterroots in 1907, but it was the election of John D. Ryan to its board of directors in 1909 that spurred the road's interest in such a possibility. Ryan was president of Anaconda Copper, BA&P's parent, and a director of two hydroelectric companies in Montana. Before the copper hauler's substations and catenary were fully in place, Albert J. Earling, CM&StP's president, approved a study of electrification between Harlowton, Mont., and Avery, Idaho. Early in 1913, he announced the decision to electrify the Three Forks-Deer Lodge, Mont., subdivision over the Rockies with a 3000-volt DC system. The completion of BA&P's electrification the next year confirmed the viability of Milwaukee's project.

At the same time, Milwaukee undertook a four-mile electrification in Great Falls, Mont., 199 miles from the main line. The project was undertaken purely as a social expedient, as the road's tracks were laid in city streets

138

By the 1940s the boxcabs had been renumbered and for the most part regrouped in three-unit sets. The color-light signals remind us that the first extensive use of such signals was along CM&StP's electrified lines. — *Milwaukee Road.*

Where steam experienced difficulties, boxcab 10211 makes its way seemingly without effort up a 2 percent grade with 55 cars near Grace, Montana, close to the Continental Divide. — *General Electric photo from Milwaukee Road.*

there. It used a small interurban-type steeple-cab locomotive operating on 1500 volts DC, and was in service from March 1915 to 1937.

The Milwaukee's first electric road locomotive, No. 10200, began to assist steam-powered trains over Pipestone Pass east of Butte in early November 1915. On the 30th of that month, electrification was formally opened over the entire distance between Three Forks and Deer Lodge, 112 miles, and full operation with electric locomotives began nine days later. A two-unit electric up front aided by an identical engine mid-train could take 3000 tons eastbound over the Rockies. Previously, two Mikados and a Mallet had been good for only 2000 tons, and at much lower speed.

In April 1916 the electric operation began on the subdivision east from Three Forks across the Belts to Harlowton, and by November the boxcab motors were purring along the Clark Fork River and around Adair Loop down into Avery, 440 miles!

An immediate effect of opening the electrification to Harlowton was that Three Forks was phased out as an engine-change point and its shop was closed. Similar economies occurred when the electrics reached Avery. Eliminating three steam locomotives per train in helper districts and operating

longer, faster trains resulted in many engine and train-crew personnel being furloughed. Conditions became much better for those who remained; the electrics' cabs were warmer, visibility was superior to that from a steam engine, smoke was absent from the tunnels, and the trip was quicker.

Speed was important to the railway as well. Running times for freight trains between Deer Lodge and Harlowton were reduced by approximately six hours, and results were similar when the Missoula Division (Deer Lodge to Avery) was electrified.

The class EF1 motors introduced regenerative braking. The traction motors became generators, creating electrical energy which was fed into the trolley system while holding the descending train in check. (Dynamic brakes on diesels today operate on the same principle except the energy they generate is dissipated as heat.) Regeneration took over most of the braking, so the air brakes were always available in an emergency, a decided safety factor. The savings in wear on brake shoes, wheels, and the air brake system were substantial. What an aid and comfort it was to enginemen! It certainly prevented a considerable amount of gray hair, high blood pressure, and ulcers.

Positioning the electric helper in the middle of the train, compared with

placing of steam pushers at the rear, resulted in much smoother handling with less slack action and fewer break-in-twos. The electrics' better tracking qualities reduced rail and bridge maintenance costs. Exactly the opposite of steam, the motors became more efficient as the temperature dropped.

Against these advantages was the extremely high cost of constructing the electrified system: poles, catenary, substations, and the financial obligations — the cost of money. The light traffic on the line eventually proved unable to support those costs.

Almost immediately, though, the road decided to also electrify over the Saddle and Cascade ranges in Washington between Othello and Tacoma, 207 miles. This zone opened for full operation in March 1920; electric helpers began to be used approximately three months earlier. Milwaukee was the proud owner of the world's longest electrified railroad: 647 route miles!

Nine miles of the branch between Black River and downtown Seattle became available to motors in July 1927, marking the final expansion of CM&StP's electrification. From 1910 to 1930 the road also operated about 15 route miles of electric interurban railway between Bozeman and Salesville (now Gallatin Gateway), Mont., first as the Gallatin Valley Railway and later as an integral part of the Milwaukee Road.

The long-distance electrification quickly became the object of attention throughout the world. Representatives from the railways of western Europe and Japan traveled to Tacoma and Deer Lodge to gain firsthand knowledge of this brilliant star of the rail world. One of the early observers was Secretary Mauduit of the French Railway Commission who was impressed with the 3000-volt system. Over the years, many Japanese not only studied the Milwaukee's epochal achievement but also welcomed CMStP&P electrical engineer Laurence Wylie into their homes when he visited Japan.

Numerous studies were made of the feasibility of electrifying the line between Avery, Idaho, and Othello, Wash. This section, at times the independent Idaho division and at other times part of the Coast division, posed the complication of alternative main lines: for passenger trains via Spokane, involving trackage rights over Union Pacific; and for freight trains via Malden, Wash. Neither line was heavily trafficked. One plan contemplated the use of multiple-unit cars for local passenger service via Malden. A final plan, about 1970, would have energized the gap as part of a total upgrading and changeover of the electrification to alternating current.

The Montana electrification was accomplished with one type of engine: two-unit, semipermanently coupled boxcab machines. Each unit had a two-axle idler truck beneath the cab end, with the rest of the carbody carried on a pair of two-axle powered frames, giving each unit a 2-B + B wheel arrangement. The carbodies floated on the running gear and did not carry any draw-

The best thing that happened to the electrification was the acquisition of the Little Joes. The first of the class, E70, and a partner use their combined 10,220 horsepower to move a train near Vendome, Montana. — *Milwaukee Road.*

142

A westbound extra leaves Othello, Washington, in July 1959. The second unit has been shortened by removing its operator's cab and pony truck, and all units wear the orange, maroon, and black scheme introduced by the F7 diesels. — *Ron Nixon.*

bar load. The two-unit locomotives had a continuous rating of 3440 h.p. but could be worked to 4100 h.p. for one hour or a whopping 5600 h.p. for thirty minutes, demonstrating why General Electric's finest could tame the mountain grades. Thirty such two-unit motors were assigned to freight service. Twelve more carried boilers for train heating and were geared for higher speeds to pull the *Olympian* and *Columbian.* When new passenger locomotives were acquired in 1919 and 1920, the twelve EP1s were regeared and joined the EF1s working freight.

During the 1930s, some units were truncated, losing their pony truck and cab, becoming, in diesel terminology, a booster. These B units were spliced into other boxcabs to make three-unit locomotives. The road also created "lash-ups" of three 2-B + B units; four-unit combinations of both full and abbreviated boxcabs were linked together as train length and drawbar capacity increased. The 1915 box cabs were incredibly successful. Some remained in service when the electrification ended — 59 years after they first emerged from Erie.

For yard switching at Butte and Deer Lodge CM&StP acquired four off-the-shelf General Electric 70-ton steeple-cab switchers like those found on interurban lines. Three of them lasted to the very end of Milwaukee's electrification.

At the close of World War Two, Milwaukee's electrification was at its original life expectancy of thirty years. Road freight diesels had proven successful, and in 1947 the *Olympian Hiawatha* entered service, running through both electric zones behind three-unit Fairbanks-Morse Erie-builts. Would these diesels replace a system that depended on locomotives built before World War One and catenary hung from uncreosoted wood poles? They could have — but the life of the electrification was unintentionally prolonged by international events one would not have expected to influence railroading in Montana.

General Electric had constructed 20 electric freight locomotives of exceptional power and appearance for the Soviet Union. By their completion, though, the cold war between that country and the United States precluded shipment of the big motors to Russia. One of them was tested on the Rocky Mountain and Coast divisions in 1948 and acquired the nickname "Little Joe," for Joseph Stalin, premier of the Soviet Union. However, the Milwaukee Road dragged its feet and was able to purchase only 12 at the price it would have originally paid for all 20. (The others had already been acquired by the Chicago South Shore & South Bend and Brazil's Paulista Railway.)

Ten of the Joes, classed EF4, entered Rocky Mountain Division freight service, operating in pairs. They were soon handling most of the freight on that

143

At Vendome the track looped back and forth to ease the grade up to the divide. The third level of track is behind the photographer's back in this scene of an eastbound train beginning to uncoil itself as it descends toward Jefferson River Canyon. Credit Laurence Wylie for the GP9, controlled from the lead Joe, providing just enough extra horsepower so the train will not have to double the grades. — *Milwaukee Road.*

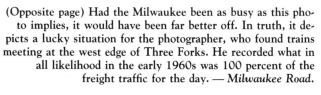

(Opposite page) Had the Milwaukee been as busy as this photo implies, it would have been far better off. In truth, it depicts a lucky situation for the photographer, who found trains meeting at the west edge of Three Forks. He recorded what in all likelihood in the early 1960s was 100 percent of the freight traffic for the day. — *Milwaukee Road.*

In 1960 E75, E74, and a GP9 approach Superior, Montana, with train 263, at the time the road's sole Midwest-to-Puget Sound freight. — *Milwaukee Road.*

division. The remaining two were assigned to the *Olympian Hiawatha*.

A pair of Joes was sufficient for freight trains through most of the electrified territory; helpers were necessary over a few ruling grades. In the late 1950s the road found itself short of electric locomotives for helper service, since a number of boxcabs had been retired. Ever-resourceful Laurence Wylie, even though he was officially retired from his post as electrical engineer, devised a scheme by which a GP9 diesel could be operated as a third unit, controlled from the cab of the lead Joe and cut in on steep grades. The Geep obviated the need for helpers with their additional labor costs, and enabled trains to run at full tonnage over the whole route. Later Wylie refined his system to enable the dynamic brake on the diesel to work in conjunction with the regenerative feature of the electrics.

In October 1963, Milwaukee added a second West Coast freight on materially expedited schedules. Train 261, the *XL Special*, was carded between Chicago and Seattle in 55 hours, while 262, the *Thunderhawk*, its eastbound counterpart, required somewhat longer. The new trains ran with four GP30s or five GP9s and at first spurned electric assistance, but it was found advantageous to enlarge upon Wylie's idea and place one Joe ahead of the diesels in

either direction. This practice continued after second-generation diesels arrived in the early 1970s — but SD40-2s and contemporary General Electric U-boats brought an end to the electrification in Washington in 1972.

Once again there were rumors of cessation of the Rocky Mountain Division electrified operation. This time they were based on substance. Early in 1973, CMStP&P announced its intention to terminate the electrification. On the morning of June 15, 1974, the final electrically powered road job came into Deer Lodge: two Joes and two SD40-2s. The road's last electric operation ended in the next morning's darkness when a 70-ton switcher (class of 1919) folded its pantograph.

There is a happy memorial to all of this. The Milwaukee Road had the sense of history to store the first boxcab inside the Deer Lodge roundhouse, where it remained until 1977. Then the decision was made to restore it and donate it to the Lake Superior Museum of Transportation at Duluth, Minnesota. With parts welded on to preclude removal by collectors, No. E50 was moved under railroad police guard to Milwaukee Shops. In early fall 1977, it was escorted to Duluth looking virtually as it did 62 years earlier as No. 10200. It was formally presented to the museum in November 1977.

DIESEL FREIGHT TRAINS

Electro-Motive's first road freight locomotive, FT demonstrator 103, began its nationwide tour in November 1939 and appeared on the Milwaukee Road during 1940, just as the final ten S2 Northerns were arriving from Baldwin Locomotive Works. The Milwaukee Road took delivery of its first FT, a four-unit locomotive numbered 40, in October 1941.

As was the case with the road's first EMD passenger locomotive, E6 No. 15, received a month earlier, the new machine was acquired with a specific duty in mind: operation of "electric-sized" trains across the non-electrified gap between the Coast Division at Othello, Washington, and the Rocky Mountain Division at Avery, Idaho. Neither the N3 2-6-6-2s nor the two class S1 4-8-4s could haul as much tonnage across the Idaho panhandle and eastern Washington as the sturdy boxcab electrics brought into Othello from the west. A second FT, No. 41, came to the twisting, turning, roller-coaster division not quite two years later.

In 1944 the war situation improved and additional FTs became available. The Milwaukee received six more of the prized machines. It would have liked more but had to settle for ten S3 4-8-4s, its final steam power.

One important assignment of these wartime diesels was replacing class L3 USRA heavy Mikados between Milwaukee and Kansas City, Missouri. The diesels could lift 4200 tons up the grade out of the Rock River valley from Beloit to Clinton Junction, Wisconsin, at 35 mph.

The FTs were dark gray with an orange stripe. Many people feel that livery was the Milwaukee's best-looking freight-diesel paint scheme. After 1950 the FTs began to receive the orange-maroon-black combination introduced that year. Earlier in their careers, the FTs had been given red warning lights in the lower portion of their noses in place of the word "Road," leaving simply "The Milwaukee" on the silver wings that decorated the nose. All the FTs were traded in on GP9s in 1959.

CMStP&P acquired a substantial fleet of F7s, several of which remained in service until 1980. The first of them were actually transition units, produced briefly by EMD between the F3 and F7 models and sometimes designated "F5." A few months later, in the spring of 1949, the first true F7s arrived in the gray paint scheme used on the FTs. Later batches of F7s introduced the orange-maroon-black paint scheme ultimately worn by all the F7s. Later, when second-generation units had demoted the Fs to trains of lesser importance, the color scheme was simplified to orange and black.

The F7s were joined by the final cab-unit model, the F9. At first, the F9s were numbered in the same series as the F7s, resulting in locomotives consisting of two models. For example, 86A was an F7A and 86B was an F7B, both 1500 h.p. units, but 86C and 86D were an F9B and an F9A, respectively, each rated at 1750 h.p. In 1959 the F9s were assigned their own number series as part of a general diesel renumbering.

F7s and F9s went everywhere the FTs did, and to some places the FTs did not. They ran to Sioux City and Sioux Falls, up the Superior Division to

The first F7s continued the livery introduced on No. 40: dark gray with an orange stripe edged in yellow. Number 78, shown at Bensenville, has had its number boxes set off with silver paint, not a standard treatment. — *Jim Scribbins.*

As time came for shopping, the FTs were repainted in the 1950 paint scheme, and most received a single number box below the headlight or improvised number indicators on either side ahead of the classification lights. Number 45, shown eastbound at La Crosse, is unusual in having F7-style number boxes and lights. The caboose and the 1934 branchline combine are for the mixed train to Austin, Minnesota. — *Cecil Cook.*

The Southeastern was dieselized with F7s, some of which were delivered with coupler covers and the running-Indian emblem. — *Bob Borcherding*.

northern Michigan, and down the Southeastern to the Indiana coalfields.

The Milwaukee purchased diesels from all the major builders except Lima. It was quick to adopt the road-switcher concept and acquired a pair of Alco RS-1s, 1678 and 1679, in 1941. The two operated for the most part on the Metaline Falls line north from Spokane, but were sold to the Army within a year to help the war effort. The road acquired a few more RS-1s during and after the war, then bought 22 RSC-2s because their 6-axle, 4-motor configuration was well suited to branch lines with light rail and bridges.

The first totally dieselized districts — the Iowa & Dakota Division from Mitchell, South Dakota, west to Rapid City; the Sioux City-Mitchell-Aber-deen line; and the Wisconsin Valley line from New Lisbon to Woodruff — were entrusted to passenger and freight RSC-2s built in 1946 and 1947, except for a few switchers from other builders. A half-dozen six-motor RSD-5s were Alco's final addition to the CMStP&P roster. Alco FAs and high-horsepower, six-motor, Century hood units demonstrated on the Milwaukee Road but elicited no orders.

Milwaukee Road acquired Fairbanks-Morse's first diesel locomotive, prototype H10-44 No. 1802, in 1944 and went back for more of that type as well as the successor H12-44. Milwaukee Shops later upgraded the 1000 h.p. units to 1200 h.p. Many survived until 1980, when the road abandoned all its lines

It looks like the vanquished is pushing the victor as an S2 doubleheads into Milwaukee with one of the last engines delivered in the gray scheme. The extra's passage has just caused the semaphore blade to drop. The foreground shadow is cast by the overpass of the Chicago North Shore & Milwaukee, a high-speed interurban line. — *Kalmbach Publishing Co.: A. L. Schmidt.*

The Milwaukee Road's densest traffic was on the C&M — the fast, double-track, CTC-signaled Chicago & Milwaukee line. This trio of F7s heads a freight extra in northern Illinois. A similar set of F7s leads time freight 263 west across agricultural country near Correll, Minnesota, on August 24, 1957. — *Both photos, Milwaukee Road.*

Only SW1s could be used on the eastern end of the Southern Minnesota line between Austin and La Crosse and its branch from Isinours to Caledonia because of bridge limitations, and the grades on the line required that they be used in multiple. A trio of "donkeys," as they were known to the crews, is shown at work between Preston and Isinours in January 1977. — *Stanley H. Mailer.*

Baldwin yard power drew occasional road assignments. This 1200 h.p. switcher is shown with a patrol (Milwaukee terminology for a local or way freight) on the Iowa & Dakota Division at Dickens, Iowa, in 1954. — *Don L. Hofsommer.*

west of Miles City, Montana, drastically cutting the railroad's need for motive power. FM pioneer 1802, renumbered 760, is retired at the Illinois Railway Museum at Union.

Milwaukee Road liked its FM road-switchers, H16-44s and "Junior Train Master" H-16-66s, and kept them in service after most other roads had retired their FMs. The C-Liner cab units were not as successful. When new, they took their turns between Bensenville and Harlowton on time freights 263 and 264, but they were quickly displaced by EMD units and relegated to the Superior Division, the Southeastern, and the Racine & Southwestern.

The Milwaukee used yard engines in road service throughout the diesel era. For the most part, such assignments were on local freights and on short branches. Probably the best known was the use of EMD 600 h.p. SW1 "donkeys" on the Southern Minnesota line between La Crosse, Wis., and Austin, Minn., because of bridges which in steam days could tolerate nothing heavier than a Ten-Wheeler. Even the newest switchers on the roster, the MP15ACs of 1976 and 1977, saw plenty of activity on such assignments — indeed, they came with road trucks and snowplow pilots in anticipation of travel beyond yard limits.

The Milwaukee was the first customer for EMD's SD7, and the model introduced a new livery: black top and frame and the remainder of the hood orange. The black top extended only to the lower edge of the number boxes and radiator; later the paint scheme was modified so the orange and black met about the level of the bottom of the cab window. CMStP&P adopted SDs in a big way when the SD40-2 was introduced in the early 1970s.

The road's most plentiful first-generation hood unit was the GP9 — curiously, Milwaukee had none of the previous model, the GP7. The 1,750 h.p. GP9 went everywhere on the railroad except on light branch lines which required six-axle locomotives.

Milwaukee's first second-generation diesels were Electro-Motive GP30s, but they were were unusual in that they rode on Alco trucks removed from RS-3s. Like most new Milwaukee power, they were first assigned to freights between Bensenville, Illinois, and Council Bluffs, Iowa. Later, they inaugurated fast time freights 261 and 262, the *XL Special* and the *Thunderhawk*, between Bensenville and Tacoma. By the 1970s they were used largely on sec-

The Fairbanks-Morse C-Liners worked only briefly on freights to the West Coast before being assigned to less illustrious duties in Michigan and Indiana. Brand-new No. 23 has a dynamometer car between its drawbar and time freight 263 at Montevideo, Minnesota, in August 1951. — *Bob Stacy*.

A covey of Fairbanks-Morse switchers was kept at Madison, Wisconsin, in the late 1950s. In addition to local switching they worked local freights. A pair is shown entering Madison from Janesville across the Lake Monona causeway in August 1958. It's a good opportunity to compare early (2305) and late (2322) models of the FM switcher. — *Jim Scribbins*.

An SD7 and an SD9 **move** grain hoppers through the loader at Albert City, Iowa, on the Des Moines-Spirit Lake line. Despite innovative marketing, a state branch line rehabilitation program, and the construction of, reportedly, the world's largest grain elevator, the former Des Moines Division did not survive Milwaukee's 1980 reorganization. Chicago & North Western acquired part of the line to continue rail service to Albert City. — *Milwaukee Road.*

If there was a modern equivalent of the L2 Mikado, it was the GP9, which operated all over the system. A quartet of the 1750-h.p. units is shown successively crossing the tall steel trestle between St. Maries and Plummer Junction, rolling through St. Maries, Idaho, and curving into Plummer Junction.
— *Milwaukee Road.*

An assortment of General Electric units has descended the steepest grade on the Puget Sound Extension, eastbound down the Saddle Mountains into Beverly, Washington. The Columbia River bridge is guarded by wind velocity signals — severe gusts sweeping down the river have blown freight cars off the bridge. — *Milwaukee Road.*

A sampling of second-generation units — GP40, SD40, two FP45s, and SD45 — brings train 264 into Avery, Idaho, in August 1972. Despite this formidable muscle, a Little Joe will close knuckles with No. 2057 to help with the strenuous ascent to St. Paul Pass Tunnel. — *Milwaukee Road.*

One-fourth of the road's GP30s, aided by a GP9, are in a siding with train 261 somewhere west of the Missouri River in South Dakota, waiting for a superior eastbound train. The train includes a business car and loaded trilevel auto carriers. — *Milwaukee Road.*

ondary trains, and some of their final duty was on the line to Kansas City.

CMStP&P followed the usual sequence of purchasing high-horsepower locomotives. A few GP35s were followed by GP40s in quantity. Plain SD40s were passed over, and 10 SD45s served to whet the appetite for more six-motor heavy power, which materialized in the form of 90 SD40-2s. Augmenting them were the five 3600 h.p. FP45 passenger units, which were repainted and placed in freight service when Amtrak was established.

Milwaukee acquired small groups of most General Electric models. At first the GEs worked principal trains opposite their EMD counterparts, but later they gravitated to the lines west of Avery, Idaho. Five U23Bs were bought to operate to Green Bay and on the Wisconsin Valley line, but GP38-2s took over those duties. The Soo Line takeover found the Valley — in fact, the whole railroad — powered by units from La Grange.

In the early 1970s Milwaukee Shops upgraded a number of GP9s, SD7s, and SD9s to improve the motive power situation, particularly with regard to secondary lines. All had their short hoods chopped for better visibility from the cab. The former GP9s received 2000 h.p. prime movers and were designated GP20. The six-motor units became SD10s — a Milwaukee Road designation — and had their ratings increased only 50 h.p. for electrical reasons. These improvements seem to have been inspired by Alco's rehabilitation several years earlier of a quartet of RSC-2s and by Milwaukee Shops' success in

increasing the horsepower of several Fairbanks-Morse and Alco units.

Unique to the Milwaukee were ten SDL39s, a shortened version of the SD39 with custom Flexicoil trucks, acquired to replace Alco RSC-2s on branches with extremely light rail.

Let's consider the operation of one of North America's premier time freights of the era: 261, the *XL Special.* From Bensenville it carried cars only for state of Washington destinations and was restricted to 45 cars to allow for pickups at Milwaukee, Watertown (new autos from a Janesville, Wis., plant), and St. Paul.

If space was available, the train would carry Twin Cities preference cars, "hot" or priority cars, coupled behind the empty Tacoma caboose, with a second caboose going only as far as St. Paul carrying the crew at the end of the train. At St. Paul, cars were added to the front of the train while the units were serviced at the diesel house. The outbound crew boarded the Tacoma caboose, and the train simply pulled away from the cars destined to the Twin Cities.

The longest intermediate stop was for 70 minutes at Aberdeen, S. Dak., to place the cars picked up at St. Paul in proper block order and inspect the train. At other points, five minutes were allowed for crew changes; the usual time for a 500-mile inspection was twenty-five minutes. At Harlowton, a Little Joe freight motor was added to the diesels for the trip across the Belts,

157

One unit train deserves mention for its special equipment, unit coal trains 780 and 781, between a mine at Gascoyne, North Dakota, and a power plant at Big Stone City, South Dakota, on a short branch north from the main line. The cars had lids to prevent the dust from their lignite coal polluting the atmosphere during transit. Special appliances at the loading and emptying sites automatically opened and closed the covers. The train is shown rolling east through McIntosh, N. Dak., behind SD40s. Four box cars behind the diesels compromise the "unit" nature of the train. The arms that open and close the covers are evident. The automated loading and unloading procedure also mandated a long underframe on the two cabooses assigned to the service. — *Both photos, Jim Scribbins.*

Rockies, and Bitteroots to Avery. At Plummer Jct., Idaho, the Spokane cars were set out at 8:45 the second morning out of Bensenville — the first time since Aberdeen that the consist had been altered. At Marengo, another block was set out for forwarding via Union Pacific to Portland. Cars for Seattle were set out at Black River; they were in Seattle at 8 p.m., 55½ hours from Bensenville. Train 261 tied up at Tacoma's Tide Flats Yard at 9 p.m.

Train 261 would not handle tank cars, flat cars without bulkheads, or gondolas loaded higher than the side of the car. The train was limited to 75 cars and 4000 tons from Watertown, Wis., to St. Paul. West of St. Paul, it was held to 60 cars and 3200 tons. Four high-horsepower diesel units ran to Tacoma from Bensenville, and, thanks to Laurence Wylie's creativity, a Little Joe could lead them across the Rocky Mountain division. In 1968, high horsepower meant primarily GP40s but General Electric U25B, U28B, and U30B units occasionally made the long run. Seven sets of power were needed to provide for 261 and its somewhat slower eastbound counterpart, 262, since a round trip between Bensenville and Tacoma required one week.

Near the end of 1974 train numbering was changed to a three-digit system. No longer would two or more trains have the same number. Further, the new numbers designated the type of train and its general operating area. Since by then most freight trains operated as extras, the numbers were actually symbols rather than train numbers.

The Chicago, Milwaukee, St. Paul & Pacific had just entered its third bankruptcy when this lash-up led a southbound freight between Hilbert and Chilton, Wisconsin. The road's future was as cold as the weather. — *Stanley H. Mailer*.

The first digit of the number was the division. The Chicago division, comprising the former Terre Haute division and the Illinois district of the old Dubuque & Illinois division, received digit 1. Interdivision trains were designated with a 2. Digits 3 through 9 were assigned respectively to the Iowa; Milwaukee; La Crosse; Iowa, Minnesota & Dakota; Aberdeen; Rocky Mountain; and Coast divisions.

The second and third digits identified the type of train: 01 through 29 for time freights, 30 through 79 for local and branchline freights, and 80 through 89 for unit trains. Extras not provided for in the Freight Train Manual were given numbers 98 and 99.

Even numbers indicated eastbound and odd numbers westbound trains as before. In the 1980s the road shifted to northbound (odd numbers) and southbound (even) designations on most subdivisions.

Unknowingly forecasting the prominence of container traffic, the Milwaukee entered intermodal operation by adopting New York Central's Flexivan system in 1958, but gradually converted to the conventional trailer-on-flatcar system. In 1966 the road inaugurated the first all-piggyback train between Chicago and the Twin Cities. The Federal Railroad Administration sponsored intermodal "Sprint" trains between Bensenville and St. Paul between 1978 and 1980. Thereafter the Milwaukee continued the service unassisted, running three trains a day with a ten-hour running time.

159

GLOSSARY AND GAZETTEER

Old names die hard on a railroad, particularly in conversational use. The Sturtevant, Wisconsin-Kittredge, Illinois, line became the Second District of the Milwaukee Division about 1930, but it is still referred to as the "Southwestern." Soo Line's Watertown Sub from Milwaukee to Portage will probably be called "the La Crosse Division" for another two decades. Soo Line, perhaps acknowledging the persistence of old names, uses "C&M Sub" as the official name of the Chicago-Milwaukee route, the former First Subdivision of the Milwaukee Division.

Railroad place names are a matter of precision. The junction 4 miles east of Ottumwa, Iowa — 4 miles east of the *station* at Ottumwa — where lines diverged to Cedar Rapids and Davenport had a name: Rutledge. The place appears on no highway maps and has no population, but it was important to the workings of the Milwaukee Road. The same was true of Kittredge, Ill., between Forreston and Lanark, and Bardwell, Wis., where the Southwestern crossed the Rondout-Janesville line.

Ashdale Cutoff: bypass around Savanna, Ill., built in 1903 as part of the Kansas City Cutoff; abandoned 1952.

Avery, Idaho: west end of the Montana electrification, at the base of the Bitterroot Mountains. Originally North Fork; renamed for Avery Rockefeller.

Calmar, Iowa: junction between the Iowa & Dakota Division (Marquette, Iowa, to Rapid City, South Dakota) and the Iowa & Southern Minnesota Division. Iowa Division trains from Marion, Iowa, terminated here, running over the Iowa & Dakota Division from Jackson Junction, 11 miles west.

C&M: informal designation for the line between Chicago and Milwaukee, from its earlier division name.

Canton, South Dakota: Junction of the Sioux City-Sioux Falls-Madison, S. Dak., route and the Marquette, Iowa-Rapid City route (both parts of the Iowa & Dakota Division).

Centralized Traffic Control (CTC): a traffic control system whereby train movements are directed through remote control of switches and signals from a central control panel. The trains operate on the authority of signal indications instead of on the authority of a timetable and train orders.

Chicago & Council Bluffs Division: earliest name for the Chicago-Marion-Council Bluffs route; actually two divisions, C&CB in Illinois and C&CB in Iowa.

Chicago, Milwaukee & Puget Sound: name of the unified components of the Mobridge, S. Dak.-Tacoma extension from 1909 to 1912.

Chicago, Milwaukee & St. Paul: name of the railway from 1874 to 1927.

Chicago, Milwaukee, St. Paul & Pacific: company's name from 1928 until acquisition by the Soo Line in 1985.

Chicago, Terre Haute & Southeastern: Milwaukee Road's Indiana line, operated as the Terre Haute Division, in 1921, and merged in 1948.

Coach: the most universal passenger car, in which passengers sit in double seats on each side of a central aisle.

Coast Division: after about 1930, all lines west of Othello, Washington. At times the Coast Division included lines between Othello and Avery, Idaho; at other times that territory was the Idaho Division.

Coupon ticket: a paper passenger ticket composed of individual segments or coupons for each section of a trip, with the coupons arranged in a single strip rather than in a booklet. It was most often used for interline trips; for example, the first coupon might be for a trip on the Milwaukee Road from the origin station to Chicago; the second for transfer between stations in Chicago; and the third for a trip from Chicago to Detroit on the Michigan Central. Coupons could have either a preprinted station or a blank where the ticket agent stamped or wrote the station name.

Davenport, Rock Island & Northwestern: railroad owned jointly by the Milwaukee Road and the Chicago, Burlington & Quincy. It formed the Clinton-Davenport, Iowa, portion of CMStP&P's Kansas City line and owned the Crescent Bridge across the Mississippi River and a line east to Moline, Ill., also used by the Milwaukee Road. Its initials (DRI) gave it the nickname "Dry Line."

Dispatcher: person overseeing the movement of trains and issuing train orders. The function is analogous to that of an airline traffic controller, but the dispatcher is a railroad employee, not a federal employee.

Dormitory car: a passenger car containing sleeping accommodations for dining and lounge car crew. Milwaukee Road dormitory cars were of the baggage-dormitory and coach-dormitory configuration.

Dubuque & Illinois Division: formed about 1930 from the Illinois Division (Chicago to Savanna) and the Dubuque Division.

Dubuque Division: the route along the west side of the Mississippi River from Samoa, Iowa (opposite Savanna), to River Junction, Minnesota (opposite La Crosse). Combined with the Illinois Division about 1930 to form the Dubuque & Illinois Division.

Embargo of 1980: the cessation of operation without abandonment of many segments of the Milwaukee Road with the approval of the reorganization court, to reduce the road to a viable route structure. The embargoed lines were later abandoned or sold to other operators.

Erie-built: Fairbanks-Morse diesel road locomotives (2000 h.p., A1A-A1A wheel arrangement, cab and booster configuration) that were built for FM by General Electric at Erie, Pennsylvania, from 1945 to 1949, because FM's Beloit, Wis., plant was working at capacity building switchers.

Green signals: green lights or flags (cloth or metal) displayed on the locomotive of a regularly scheduled train to indicate that another section of that train is following. (White lights or flags on the locomotive indicate an extra train, one not listed in the timetable.)

Harlowton, Montana: east end of the Montana electrification, meeting point of the Trans-Missouri Division (east of Harlowton) and the Rocky Mountain Division (west), and junction with the Northern Montana line. Originally named Merino, the town was renamed to honor Montana Railroad owner Richard Harlow. Boxcab E57B is on display in a city park there.

Idaho & Washington Northern: line from Spokane to Metaline Falls, Wash. Much of it survives in 1989 as the Pend Oreille Valley Railroad.

Idaho Division: all lines between the two electrified zones, at times incorporated into the Coast Division.

Illinois Division: the Chicago-Savanna-East Moline route, later part of the Dubuque & Illinois Division.

Indiana Harbor Belt Railroad: a Chicago terminal railroad owned in recent years by the Milwaukee Road and Conrail. Conrail's share was inherited from New York Central; Chicago & North Western was also an owner until 1961. The Milwaukee Road used the IHB for access to the Terre Haute Division.

Iowa & Dakota Division: lines from Marquette, Iowa, to Rapid City, S. Dak.; Sioux City-Sioux Falls-Madison, S. Dak.; Sioux City-Mitchell, S. Dak.; and branches from those lines.

Iowa & Minnesota line: the line from Calmar, Iowa, through Austin, Minn., to St. Paul and Minneapolis. It had division status until about 1930.

Iowa & Southern Minnesota Division: formed about 1930 from the Iowa & Minnesota Division and the Southern Minnesota Division (La Crosse, Wis.-Wessington Springs, S. Dak.), plus branches.

Iowa Division: lines from Savanna, Ill., through Manilla, Iowa, to Council Bluffs; from Manilla to Sioux City; Marion to Jackson Junction; Des Moines to Spirit Lake; and branches from those lines.

J Line: the subdivision of the Milwaukee Division extending from Rondout, Ill., to Janesville, Wis. (Don't confuse it with the "J," the Elgin, Joliet & Eastern Railway, which crosses the Milwaukee Road at Rondout.)

Kansas City Cutoff: a combination of new lines (Ashdale-Ebner, Ill., and Muscatine-Rutledge, Iowa), existing track (Ebner-East Moline, Ill.), and trackage rights (on Davenport, Rock Island & Northwestern and Chicago, Rock Island & Pacific between East Moline and Muscatine). It was opened in 1903 from Ashdale to Rutledge (just east of Ottumwa) to replace a more circuitous route through Marion, Iowa.

Kansas City Division: lines from Davenport to Kansas City and from Cedar Rapids to Rutledge, Iowa.

La Crosse & River Division: formed about 1930 from the La Crosse, River, and Wisconsin Valley divisions. It comprised the main line from Milwaukee to the Twin Cities, the Wisconsin Valley line north from New Lis-

bon, Wis., and branch lines from Watertown and Portage to Madison, Wis.

Ladd, Illinois: southern operating terminal of the line from Janesville south through Rockford, Ill., to several cities in the Illinois River valley.

Lines East: everything east of Mobridge, S. Dak., plus the Rapid City line — everything but the Puget Sound Extension.

Lines West: the Puget Sound Extension; all lines west of Mobridge, S. Dak., except the Chamberlain-Rapid City, S. Dak., route.

Mallet: an articulated steam locomotive with high-pressure and low-pressure cylinders; sometimes (erroneously) any articulated locomotive.

Markers: lamps or flags (cloth or metal) displayed at the rear of a train. The display of markers confers train status.

Marquette, Iowa: Intersection of the Dubuque line with the Madison, Wis.-Rapid City, S. Dak., line. Marquette was connected with Prairie du Chien, Wis., by a pontoon (floating) bridge.

Menomonee Valley: industrial district of the city of Milwaukee, location of Milwaukee Shops, Airline and Muskego yards, and several other Milwaukee Road facilities.

Milwaukee & Mississippi: Milwaukee Road's earliest operating predecessor, in existence 1850-1861.

Milwaukee Shops: the road's principal shops, established in 1878. The shops built and maintained locomotives and passenger and freight cars. They were originally known as West Milwaukee Shops.

Mixed train: a train carrying both freight and passengers, usually operating on branches and secondary lines, and designated as such in the operating timetable.

Missoula Division: Deer Lodge, Mont.-Avery, Idaho; became part of Rocky Mountain Division after electrification.

Northern Division: the first route from Milwaukee to Portage, via Horicon (also called the Old Line). It became the Third District of the Milwaukee Division about 1930.

Northern Iowa line: recent designation for the Marquette-Sheldon, Iowa-Canton, S. Dak., route.

Northern Montana: Harlowton-Lewistown-Great Falls line and branches. It had division status until it was merged into the Rocky Mountain Division.

Map from Milwaukee Road passenger timetable, May 25, 1942.

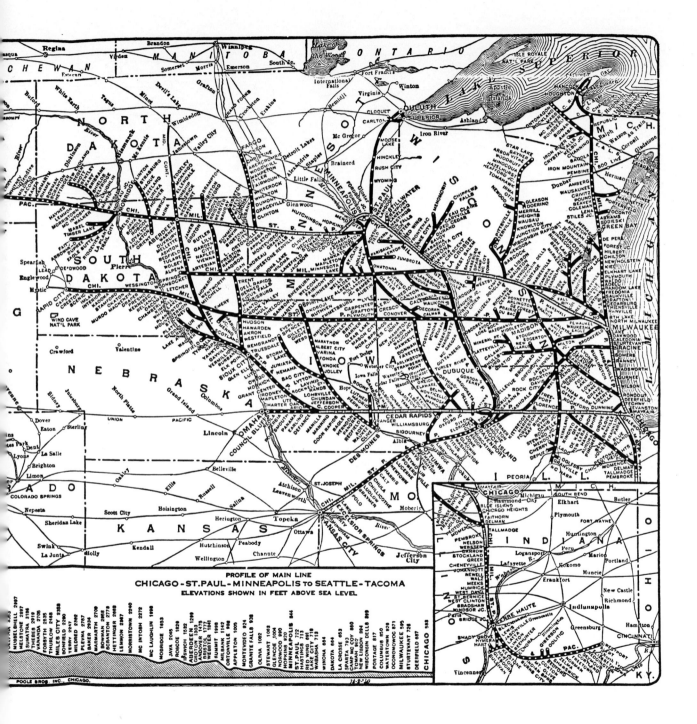

PROFILE OF MAIN LINE
CHICAGO - ST. PAUL - MINNEAPOLIS to SEATTLE - TACOMA
ELEVATIONS SHOWN IN FEET ABOVE SEA LEVEL

POOLE BROS. INC., CHICAGO.

163

Othello, Washington: east end of the Washington electrification; demarcation between the Coast and Idaho divisions.

Parlor car: passenger car for daytime first-class travel, with single revolving, reclining armchairs on each side of the aisle.

Prairie du Chien Division: the line from Milwaukee through Janesville, Madison, and Prairie du Chien, Wis., to Marquette, Iowa. It was combined with the Mineral Point Division (lines running west from Janesville) to form the Madison Division about 1930. It was later part of the La Crosse Division.

Puget Sound: nickname of the Chicago, Milwaukee & Puget Sound.

Puget Sound Extension: the line from Mobridge, S. Dak., to Seattle and Tacoma, Wash., constructed between 1906 and 1909.

Railway Post Office (RPO): a passenger train car or a portion of a car equipped for sorting mail and staffed by postal employees. RPO cars had catcher arms that could pick up mailbags at speed from trackside cranes. (Discharging mail at speed was simply a matter of tossing the bag out the door.)

Rocky Mountain Division: originally the line from Harlowton to Deer Lodge, Mont.; later it absorbed the Missoula Division (Deer Lodge-Avery) and the Northern Montana Division (Harlowton-Great Falls).

Rotary snowplow: a snowplow with a rotating fanlike blade which hurls snow to the side of the track.

St. Paul: nickname for the Chicago, Milwaukee & St. Paul, one used more by the public than by the railway.

Savanna, Illinois: Mississippi River town at the intersection of the Chicago-Council Bluffs, Milwaukee-Kansas City, and Dubuque lines; fourth-busiest yard on the system.

Set-out sleeper: A sleeping car parked in a station for occupancy either before departure or after arrival of a train, so passengers can retire or rise at a decent hour. For example, passengers could board the *Pioneer Limited*'s Milwaukee-Minneapolis car at 9 p.m. and go to sleep knowing that train 1 would pick up the car at 12:55 a.m. On the return trip, the car was dropped at Milwaukee at 6 a.m., and passengers could remain aboard till 8.

Southeastern: informal name for the Terre Haute Division, from its origin as the Chicago, Terre Haute & Southeastern Railway.

Southern Minnesota: one-time division which extended from La Crosse, Wis., to Wessington Springs, S. Dak., and from Madison, S. Dak., north to Bristol, S. Dak.

Southwestern: informal name for the Sturtevant, Wis.-Kittredge, Ill., line. It was for a long time the Racine & Southwestern Division; it became the Second District of the Milwaukee Division about 1930.

Superior Division: secondary main line from Milwaukee to the upper peninsula of Michigan. It was merged into the Milwaukee Division about 1950.

Interior, 1937 *Hiawatha* parlor car. — *Milwaukee Road.*

Tacoma Eastern Railroad: independent line from Tacoma, Wash., south to Morton and Ashford. It was acquired by the CM&PS in 1910 and merged by the CM&StP in 1919.

Terre Haute Division: operating designation for the Chicago, Terre Haute & Southeastern.

Tourist car: a sleeping car with upper and lower berths priced less than those in first-class sleepers and in which, usually, an intermediate rail fare (between coach and first class) was charged. Milwaukee designated its streamlined tourist sleepers (the only ones in the U. S.) "Touralux."

United States Railroad Administration (USRA): federal agency directing the operation of U. S. railroads during and shortly after World War One.

Valley or

Wisconsin Valley: the secondary main line extending north from New Lisbon, Wis., almost to the Michigan border. Once a separate division, it became the Third District of the La Crosse & River Division about 1930.

INDEX

In 1951 a work train heads out of Bovill, Idaho, toward Elk River to pick up logs that have fallen off trains. The track in the foreground belongs to the Washington, Idaho & Montana Railway.
— *Philip R. Hastings*.